"Cheri gives us a much-needed resource for children who struggle with written expression, and for the parents and teachers who work with them. Her unique and in-depth perspective sheds new light on a very misunderstood phenomenon."
-Cristina Urban, MS, OTR/L,
parent of a child with dysgraphia

"An eye-opening resource! Cheri presents the information in such an understandable and flowing manner for parents, teachers, and therapists. She breaks down and explains the types of dysgraphia with the focus on building those "neural pathways". I also appreciate her transparency with sharing her own struggles."
-Jorge Ochoa, OTR/L

Cheri is an exceptional speaker and a very good communicator. Truly enjoyed her presentation and everyone was enlightened by her knowledge of Dysgraphia. Working on a hands-on activity during her speech set the learning process in motion for the group. We will invite Cheri back.
-Andee Swoyer, Community leader

Handwriting
Brain-Body
DisConnect

Handwriting
Brain-Body
DisConnect

Adaptive teaching techniques to unlock a child's dysgraphia for the classroom and at home

CHERI DOTTERER, MS, OTR/L

Disclaimer: I am not a physician. I have been a rehab professional for over 20 years. This book is a result of seeing teachers strain to manage their classroom due to that one student in the classroom that demands more time than they have to offer and so many parents' dreams shattered because the school said, "No, your child does not qualify" for services or "we don't know how to accommodate your child." I was one of those parents and am a direct service provider for the school system. Seeing a child struggle in school is one of the most difficult parts of being a teacher or parent. The material that is provided in this book is for your general knowledge. Consult your local physician, healthcare professionals, school professionals, and related service providers before considering a diagnosis of dysgraphia for a child.

Printed in the United States of America.
Published by Author Academy Elite
P.O. Box 43, Powell, OH 43055
www.AuthorAcademyElite.com

Paperback: 978-1-64085-571-7
Hardback: 978-1-64085-392-8
E-book: 978-1-64085-393-5
Library of Congress Control Number: 2018953205

Dotterer, Cheri L. | Marzili, Alyssa, illustrator.

Handwriting Brain-Body DisConnect: Adaptive teaching techniques to unlock a child's dysgraphia for the classroom and at home / by Cheri L. Dotterer; illustrated by Alyssa Marzili.

Powell, OH: Author Academy Elite, 2018. | Analysis of the Types of Dysgraphia with teaching strategies to correlate with the education system.

LCCN 2018953205 (print) | Paperback: 978-1-64085-391-1 |

Hardback: 978-1-64085-392-8 | E-book: 978-1-64085-393-5

BISAC: EDU029070 | Education/Teaching Methods & Materials/Language Arts

Amazon: Teaching | Teacher Resources | Special Education | Learning Disabilities

LC record available at https://lccn.loc.gov/2018953205

Dedication

This book is dedicated to all the children who suffer from handwriting problems like dysgraphia and the educators, related service providers, and parents teaching them how to be successful citizens of society.

Table of Contents

Part Three

Part Four

Appendices

List of Illustrations

List of Tables

Foreword

In her famous TED talk, the late Rita Pierson said, "Every child deserves a champion; an adult who will never give up on them, who understands the power of connection and insists that they become the best they can possibly be." In *Handwriting Brain-Body Disconnect*, Cheri Dotterer makes it clear that she is that champion as she navigates you through the maze of dysgraphia.

This journey of understanding took Cheri many years, so you are not left to figure this it out on your own. Her personal insight and practical advice ensure you won't go it alone. Cheri shares her story about how she personally navigated this process. She's lived it. Now she makes sure you know exactly what steps to take.

This book is about more than finding a way to help with dysgraphia. It's about finding a way for all of us to work through our "invisible challenges." Unlocking dysgraphia is just a result when you care for those you serve.

Cheri's content is clear, concise, and an easy read for parents, and it's packed with content for therapists and teachers. Cheri wants you to see results, and these steps will get you there.

I'm excited for you because in my conversations with Cheri about learning differences, I know the content in this book will give you the answers you've been seeking. As an educator for over 20 years, I am passionate about finding ways for all children to learn. I believe this content will give parents hope that their children will be able to do far above what they even believed possible.

Anita M. McLaurin, M. Ed.
Specialty Curriculum Design and Development
Author of *My Father Said I Could*

Preface

Definition, Audience, and Purpose

There is a misconception about dyslexia, dysgraphia, and dyscalculia. Some people use the terms interchangeably. Simply put:

dyslexia is defined as difficulty with reading;
dysgraphia is defined as difficulty with writing;
dyscalculia is defined as difficulty with math concepts.

Each topic is much more complicated. This book is written for teachers, parents, occupational therapists transitioning to school-based practice, and other related service professionals. The focus will be on dysgraphia. If you want information on dyslexia and dyscalculia, please refer to other resources.

Acknowledgements

It takes a village to support dysgraphia.
It also takes a village to write a book.

My husband, Jeffrey L Dotterer: Without your support, this project would have never come to pass. I love you!

My children, Krista and Michael: Thank you for being a sounding board for my crazy ideas. I love you!

My mom and dad, Gary and Janet Yerger: You have always encouraged me to do be the best that I could be. Thank you! I love you!

Mary Lawson: This project would have never gotten started without our conversations over IEPs, sensory processing disorders, and educational advocacy.

My developmental editor, William Houlette: Thank you for helping me take my scattered thoughts and pin point the content for this book.

My content editor, Bethany Peat: Thank you for your organizational skills and aligning my content with the educator.

My illustrator, Allyssa Marzili: You are an amazing artist!

Anita Marye McLaurin: Thank you for awesome foreword!

Cristina Urban, Jorge Ochoa, and Andee Swoyer for your amazing endorsements of this book.

My publisher, Kary Oberbrunner: Your training and guidance was worth every moment of mentoring you provide.

My students and their parents who made me realize that there was a gap that needed clarification in the research regarding dysgraphia. Thank you for understanding that I am keeping your names confidential.

Beverly Moskowitz, my OT Mom: You got my heart prepared for this adventure.

Kerri Hample, Karen Cameron, and Sue O'Neill for keeping my content true to the *Occupational Therapy Practice Framework, third edition.*

Bethany Geisinger: Thank you for reviewing the first draft and supporting me in completing this project over the last several years.

October is Dyslexia Awareness Month

"This is a time for parents, educators, and policymakers to understand how these disabilities impact students and their families, to reflect on the significant achievements that these students have made, and to renew our commitment to creating a stronger future for them (Duncan, 2015)."

– Arne Duncan, Secretary of Education 2009-2015

"This LD Awareness Month, I encourage all teachers to consider which of their students might have dyslexia. ...Help them to identify and celebrate their interests and strengths. ...I urge all students with learning disabilities to pursue activities that you enjoy. Believe in your ability to learn. Use your voice to increase awareness and understanding of the whole of dyslexia (Erickson, 2015)."

– McKenzie Erickson, US Department of Education

Introduction

How many times have you heard this?

"I can't! I can't! I just CAN'T do it, Mom (or Dad)!"

That sentence is then followed by an awful temper tantrum. How many nights do you sit around the homework table? The homework doesn't get done and you are writing yet another letter to the teacher, saying...

"We tried. He refused. She refused."

Like so many parents, I have experienced working long after bedtime to get homework done.

My daughter was an avid reader, but she will tell you to this day that she cannot spell. While she was in grade school, we found some ways to help her remember, but they were not always successful.

My son, on the other hand has atrocious handwriting. As an occupational therapist, I regularly work with clients to develop proper handwriting skills. I tried many accommodations with my son, but he refused them all. Refusal to write or have accommodations for writing is common when dealing with someone who has dysgraphia. I have not only seen these problems in my children, but also in the clients that I treat each day.

According to the Dyslexia Literacy and Clinical Services Foundation (Dyslexia Literacy and Clinical Services (SPELD), 2014), **written expression** is defined as the "acquisition of fluent and efficient writing skills." Dysgraphia is defined by the International Dyslexia Association (IDA) as "a condition of impaired letter writing by hand" (Berninger & Wolf, 2018). The inability to write efficiently is a glitch in the sensory-motor processing neural pathway. This glitch in the processing creates frustration, excessive erasing, associated or extra motor responses, and the need to start over frequently. Dysgraphia may occur alongside dyslexia or alone. Extra motor responses are movements that occur alongside a movement but are not required for the movement to occur. An example is sticking your tongue out when writing. The frustration, erasing, and motor responses impact written expression, handwriting letters and numbers, creating sentences and paragraphs. The result is a crumbled school paper and a refusal to finish the assignment, as well as a very upset child who may say, "I hate school."

I have seen these challenges, not only as a parent and an occupational therapist, but also because I struggle with dyslexia and dysgraphia myself. I suffer from light sensitivity. That makes white paper appear like a white blob with black lines on it. Reading is still difficult if the font size is small.

Both of my children and I are twice exceptional (2e). That means that we are gifted in some areas and have a learning disability in another area. It is unclear who first coined the term. However, researchers attribute the term to James Gallagher when he began publishing articles about gifted and handicapped students in the 1970s (Pfeiffer, et al., 2015). Often the disabilities are hiding until you get to know the person. Many people have invisible challenges. Today, research helps us understand them more clearly than Gallagher did in the 1970s.

I noticed that many of my extremely smart students had handwriting difficulties also. My role as the occupational therapist was to improve the student's ability to access their education (USDOE, 2014). I sought to offer the best practices described in the professional literature. For me though, it was not only because that was my job, but was also answering that life-long question I had of "what's wrong with me?" While learning everything I could from the popular handwriting curriculums, there was still something missing.

How was a child with dysgraphia different from a child with dyslexia **and** dysgraphia? How can a child be an avid reader and not be able to write? Where does dyscalculia come into the picture? What is the missing link?

The children I observed sometimes demonstrated good visual perceptual skills and sometimes good visual motor skills. These terms are discussed later in the book. How could a child with average visual perceptual assessment scores have dysgraphia? The even more confusing scores were the visual motor assessment scores. How could a child score well here and have dysgraphia? Were there other scores or signs that helped the practitioner properly interpret the assessment results? How did these scores impact visual memory? How could I help teachers, parents, and occupational therapists to better understand the phenomenon called dysgraphia?

My quest to understand my own struggles, the quirks of my children, and the challenges of the children I see has taught me I am not alone. Neither are you. There are many children who struggle with handwriting. Teachers and parents are overwhelmed. How can a child read for hours and refuse to write anything? How can a child copy a sentence with precision, yet when you take the sample sentence away, their handwriting becomes a disaster? Literature regarding dysgraphia was vague.

Let me reinforce again, you are not alone. You will survive the day and the school year. You do not need to feel overwhelming frustration as your child begins his or her journey.

According to the Motor Learning Theory, children need to incorporate movement, visual, and auditory input to solidify their memory (Zwicker & Harris, 2009). Applying the principles of Motor Learning Theory to the Types of Dysgraphia will improve their ability retain the visual memory of letter formation and words to enhance their ability to learn. *Handwriting Brain-Body Disconnect* facilitates a multi-sensory approach to encourage writing. It teaches you how strategies to access the visual memory to strengthen the learning process.

You will read how these difficulties impacted my education throughout the book. I also share stories from clients and how writing difficulties have impacted their ability to learn.

List of Abbreviations

American Occupational Therapy Association	AOTA
American Psychological Association	APA
Attention Deficit Hyperactivity Disorder	ADHD
Central Nervous System	CNS
Chief Executive Officer	CEO
Control, Accuracy, Precision, Speed	CAPS
Diagnostic and Statistical Manual, Fifth edition	DSM-5
Dyslexia Literacy & Clinical Services	SPELD
Free Appropriate Public Education	FAPE
Handwriting without Tears	HWT
Individualized Education Plan	IEP
Individuals with Disabilities Act	IDEA
Memory Dysgraphia	MemD
Motor Dysgraphia	MotorD
Intelligence Quotient	IQ
Motor, Ocular, Vestibular, Environment, Repeat	MOVER
Non-rapid eye movement	NREM
Occupational Therapist	OT

Paragraph Formation Dysgraphia	PFD
Position in Space, Form Constancy, Orientation, Laterality, Direction	P-FOLD
Pre-frontal Cortex	PFC
Rapid eye movement	REM
Sensory Processing Disorder	SPD
Sentence Formation Dysgraphia	SFD
Size Matters Handwriting Program	SMHP
Special Education	SpEd
Speech and Language Pathologist	SLP
Traumatic Brain Injury	TBI
United States Department of Education	USDOE
Visual-Spatial Dysgraphia	VSD
Word Formation Dysgraphia	WFD

PART ONE

Dysgraphia~Decoding~Encoding

Chapter One

Dysgraphia

EMERGING WRITERS DO not always translate what they see and hear to written expression well. Approximately 10-33% of the population have handwriting hindrances (VanHoorn, Maathuis, Peters, & Hadders-Algra, 2010). Experts indicate that a child must understand directionality, recognize similarities and differences, as well as possess a functional pencil grip, and the ability to copy to have functional handwriting skills (VanHoorn, Maathuis, Peters, & Hadders-Algra, 2010). When a child is having difficulty with handwriting, it is called dysgraphia. While Behringer and Wolf (2018) define dysgraphia based on an educational classification, the *Diagnostic and Statistical Manual of Mental Disorders, fifth edition* (DSM-5) (American Psychiatric Association (APA), 2013) does not define dysgraphia as a specific identifiable diagnosis. It is mentioned as a symptom under the criterion of a Specific Learning Disability, Neurodevelopmental Disorders section.

"Dys" means disability and "graph" means to write by hand. Dysgraphia is a genetic condition, but the cause is not understood. Possible origins include a lack of oxygen or head injury (Karnik & Karnik, 2012). The following is a general list of symptoms taken from the research of Karnik and Karnik (2012). It has been paraphrased for clarity.

- Writing slower than typical students of the same age
- Odd positions of the wrist or paper
- Mixing upper and lowercase letter forms
- Inconsistency in forming letters
- Cramping fingers or hands
- Irregular letter formation, size, sequencing, or line placement
- Poor letter organization
- Unorganized thought processes when writing paragraphs
- Difficult managing margins
- Inefficient pencil pressure
- Poor spelling
- Intentionally watching their hand write letters
- Awkward pencil grasp
- Poor fine motor skills
- Avoiding writing tasks
- Letter and number reversals
- Difficulty with written expression
- Need extended time to complete tasks

Brant (2014) and Bryce & Stephens (2014) state that there are three types of dysgraphia. Karnik and Karnik (2012) indicate five different types. None of the published material provides clear explanations along with a functional application to help students cope with dysgraphia.

After much deliberation and research, I have merged the findings of the researchers to clarify the confusion regarding dysgraphia. The Types of Dysgraphia were created to reflect the developmental levels of reading and writing and interweaves them with sensory-motor development to help explain dysgraphia. Although these types are distinctly different in their symptoms, students may have overlapping symptoms from each type. Students may never develop the proper neural pathways to progress through each type. They could also develop some, but not all the neural pathways yielding splintering skills in various areas. Depending on the day, students may also have moments in which they remain in lower developmental patterns.

The foundation of dysgraphia is the ability to process information. To begin processing information, a person must be able to interpret visual-spatial information and respond to it. In this type, early reading difficulties also impact the ability to write. Visual-spatial dysgraphia (VSD) involves the sensory input a person receives from their environment. Motor Dysgraphia (MotorD) reflects the motor development of a student. The third type is Memory Dysgraphia (MemD), which reflects the brain-body disconnection to effective working memory. Working memory is the body's short-term memory system, which keeps a constant running record of what the body is doing. These types of dysgraphia involve primarily the mechanical portions of writing. Word and Sentence Formation Dysgraphia (SFD) are more greatly impacted by the language aspects of writing. Finally, Paragraph Formation Dysgraphia (PFD) utilizes our cognitive neural pathways to develop creating prose. However, our brain and body are one complete unit. All aspects of writing intermingle.

Some authors (Brant, 2014); (Bryce & Stephens, 2014) (Karnik & Karnik, 2012); & (HPS, 2018) have referred to this type of dysgraphia (difficulties with word, sentence, and paragraph formation) as dyslexic dysgraphia. However, they qualify their terminology stating that this type of dysgraphia does not reflect dyslexia (a disability in reading). This created some confusion.

Information processing is an individual's ability to learn and retain new information; that is, decode, interpret, and respond with efficiently encoded written words. it in their brains. Merriam-Webster (2017) clarifies information processing as short-term memory acquisition, working memory capacity, recall, and word fluency. Merriam (2017) also states the individuals may have auditory interferences such as loud or annoying noises distracting them from focusing on their work. A second type of interference is that of one's own thoughts distracting the individual from producing work. We've all experienced preoccupation with our internal thoughts that have nothing to do with the task we need to complete. More information on executive functioning is discussed in chapter five.

Information Processing Dysgraphia

Information Processing Dysgraphia encompasses all aspects of the mechanics, language, and cognitive aspects of writing at their most fundamental levels. Letter and number comprehension and use is the foundation of processing information. Placing the information on paper is also a concern with information processing dysgraphia. Typically, handwriting is illegible, motor skills are impaired, and language skills are laborious for the student. Working memory disruptions create hesitation and confusion with letter formation, sizing, sequencing, and line placement, and so impact the mechanical portion of writing. The language and cognitive portions of writing are engaged developmentally at a basic level.

On a brighter side, a student with information processing dysgraphia's ability to copy is wonderful. They tell oral stories in explicit detail. With that visual cue in front of them, they do not need to use their working memory to create letter or number forms. This student flourishes if they have a scribe to initially record their oral feedback. The student then recopies it. As a teacher or parent, you may also digitally record the student's information and have them write down the material if the playback contains a visual cue for letters, numbers, and any other pertinent symbols. Assistive technology has made playback much easier.

The next two forms of dysgraphia are the most understood forms. They are the types that are most common referral for occupational therapy. Developmentally, our brain-body connections take sensory feedback and create motor responses.

Visual-Spatial Dysgraphia (VSD)

Visual-Spatial Dysgraphia (VSD) is a brain-body disconnect involving a lack of visual-spatial awareness or visual perception. Without visual-spatial awareness, students cannot determine where to place the symbols on paper. These students typically have the most illegible handwriting of all the types of dysgraphia (Bryce

& Stephens, 2014). Visual-spatial awareness is the foundation of visual perception. Integration of the motor output is visual-motor integration. Visual perception and visual-motor integration will be explained further in supplemental chapters.

Students with a primary concern of visual-spatial awareness most likely have age appropriate fine motor skills. They can follow rhythmic music patterns. Their oral narration and spelling are age appropriate (Brant, 2014). They also have difficulty with drawing, coloring, painting, letter formation, and accurately creating simple shapes. Their writing speed and fluency are poor. As a result, they avoid handwriting (Bryce & Stephens, 2014); (Karnik & Karnik, 2012).

Students with VSD require a visual cue for anything that they are writing, drawing, coloring, or painting. They do well with drawings that have individual steps broken down into small steps. *RealOTSolutions.com* has a book called *I Can Draw* that breaks drawings down into 3, 4, and 5-steps (Moskowitz, 2015).

Most handwriting programs come equipped with a desktop strip that can be placed on the student's desk. These strips provide a visual cue for the program being taught.

To help a student with word and letter spacing, many sensory-motor style supports have been invented. Anything that creates a visual cue between words will help. Popsicle sticks, stickers, and fingers have been used to facilitate the cue.

Due to the gift of rhythm in these children, songs are helpful in the student's mastery of the visual-spatial difficulties. *Handwriting Without Tears* has several CDs that help students. *Real OT Solutions* also uses songs, but they have not published a CD (Olsen & Knapton, 2008).

Motor Dysgraphia (MotorD)

If the area of concern is motor in nature, MotorD is the level in which the student will have more trouble. Delays in fine motor skills, eye-hand coordination, motor clumsiness, and hand strength plague these students. Not only do they have trouble with handwriting, but they also behave differently in the hall or at recess. These students need to "hug" the wall as they are moving through the hallway. They have difficulty climbing playground equipment. They have difficulty standing on one foot. At their desk, students lean forward and lay on the desk or slouch in their chair. They complain of hand pain or cramping when writing. They use every excuse in the book to not engage in handwriting. Many students with low muscle tone have MotorD.

Additionally, they have trouble crossing midline. For example, tasks that require their arm to reach across their body to the opposite side are difficult. They contour their body in unusual ways to compensate for the need to cross midline. Letters like X force the writer to cross midline and is one reason that diagonal lines are more difficult to write for them. Writing to the end of the paper is difficult if the paper is taped on the table near their belly button. These students tend to rotate their paper rather than writing in typical letter formation movement patterns.

Karnik and Karnik (2012) state that these students tend to write extremely slow, form letter unusually, such as from the baseline up, and have difficulty properly using handwriting paper. They size letters inconsistently, demonstrate unique methods to sequence letters, and do not understand proper baseline placement of letters. Because of being unsure about letters, they tend to mix upper and lower cases. Due to their low muscle tone, they tend to write very lightly; sometimes their handwriting is so faint, it can hardly be read. On the other hand, some children write with such pressure to create dark lines, they are frequently breaking pencil tips. However, spelling and the ability to draw shapes are intact. Bryce & Stephens (2014) and Brant (2014) concur that visual-spatial tasks such as coloring, drawing, and painting are intact. Karnik and Karnik (2012) also indicate other strengths include: good auditory and visual memory, the ability to narrate responses verbally, and age appropriate spelling.

Due to the low muscle tone, occupational therapists may offer adaptive seating or pencil grips for students with MotorD. Another adaptation could include a slant board.

The motor delays will impact other tasks that students need to accomplish. These tasks may include dressing properly. If your child dresses with clothes inside out or backwards, they may have a dyspraxia. Dyspraxia is inability to "conceptualize, plan, and execute a habitual motor act" (Parham & Mailloux, 2005, p. 382). It cannot be explained through a medical diagnosis (Parham & Mailloux, 2005).

Tying shoes and opening containers tend to disrupt the lives of these children and their caregivers. See your occupational therapist for adaptive strategies to decrease awkward movement patterns.

Another task that may be awkward is using utensils. Cutting food requires a child to cross midline and use both upper extremities simultaneously. If your child is in grade school and you have given them opportunities to try using a knife and fork with little success, ask for an occupational therapy evaluation.

Hand strengthening activities and in-hand manipulation activities help these students. An example of a hand strengthening activity is pulling coins out of silly putty or play dough. Therapy putty is used more often by therapists it is gluten-free. Moving two dice around in your hand is an in-hand manipulation activity. These tasks will help improve the child's ability to hold a pencil for longer periods of time.

Students with MotorD benefit from extended time to complete assignments. They also benefit from direct copying rather than copying from the board. Encourage them to use a spacer between words. Examples of spacers include popsicle sticks, stickers, and fingers, as mentioned in the section on VSD.

Memory Dysgraphia (MemD)

A level of dysgraphia that can overlap both the visual-spatial and motor areas is MemD. This complex brain-body connection process can impact one or both the sensory and the motor systems. In addition, the working memory system may trigger levels of inefficiency.

Lack of recall or working memory is the greatest barrier for this student. They have difficulty remembering if the stick of the letter "b" is first or if the ball is first. Hence, reversals are highly prevalent in this population. Another behavior, they overwrite their letters and erase often. Many times, they rip their paper while erasing due to the frustration of knowing their letter wasn't right. They were not sure how to fix the letter. They can exhibit low muscle tone like children with MotorD, but it is their working memory that causes them the most grief. Unfamiliar words, words that do not follow phonetics rules, and words with blends are difficult (Karnik & Karnik, 2012); (HPS, 2018). Spelling is atrocious.

Unlike the child with MotorD, copying skills are intact. Their visual-spatial awareness is typically intact.

These children tend to be perfectionists. They are avid readers. They have good oral recall. It's the written expression of information that interferes with their success in school. These children tend to create the most confusion among teachers and therapists. Because they can read well, teachers expect their writing do be just as accomplished. Since their sensory-motor systems are intact, therapists tend to dismiss their deficits as if they do not qualify for services.

These children tend to fall between the cracks. This delay in working memory creates anxiety, frustration, and refusals to participate. These children are labeled "lazy." The survival mechanism and coping strategy that is created in their brain gives others that impression, but that is farthest from the truth. The survival mechanism activates the fight-flight-fright response and says, "Get outta here." The resulting behavior is refusal and as a result they are labelled "lazy." These children need your help.

Students with MemD benefit from the strategies from both visual-spatial and motor dysgraphic students. They need support to build their neural pathways and solidify the working memory. They benefit from a scribe. They can copy the scribed material onto a final copy with visual cues for all symbols.

Progressing beyond individual symbols to words involves language. The language developmental process begins with blends and syllables. Memory is the bridge between the sensory-motor system and the language and cognitive systems. The word formation level of dysgraphia integrates the use of symbols into language. Words involve the integration of the mechanical and language processes of neural development.

Once the basic sensory-motor-memory system is functioning that students can recall single letters or

numbers, the student can begin to build on single letters through writing words, sentences, and paragraphs.
It is at this point that the language portion of writing
becomes an integral part of the process.

Word Formation Dysgraphia (WFD)

Word Formation Dysgraphia (WFD) is simply difficulty in
understanding the basics of word and syllable connections. This type of dysgraphia often manifests as a lack
of proficiency in the syllabic stage of writing. More information about the syllabic stage of writing is discussed
in the next chapter. At this stage, school psychologists
and speech-language pathologists can assist the student more directly than the occupational therapist.
However, the occupational therapist should remain
part of the team as a consultant creating motor-based
strategies to assist in the word formation concepts.
Students may continue to demonstrate sensory-motor
processing immaturity in some areas. Ideal treatment
models for these students include proprioceptive, kinesthetic, and vestibular movements. Chapter six clarifies
the definitions and treatment interventions of these
terms.

Most students with WFD can read at grade level and
have good reading comprehension skills. Orally they tell
the best stories. However, when they attempt to write
answers on paper, it is like they go into slow motion.
They struggle to write letters correctly on paper. They
have reversals and spelling is dependent on phonetics
and memory skills.

If an adult scribes their words on paper, these children demonstrate superb copying skills have excellent
fine motor skills, and age appropriate oral spelling. Their
use of handwriting paper is age appropriate when

direct line copying. However, they have more difficulty copying from the board or from a book.

Sentence Formation Dysgraphia (SFD)

SFD is understanding the basics of sentence structure, syntax, and basic grammar skills. Writing meaningful sentence and organizing their thoughts on paper is daunting. Their use of grammar fluctuates. One moment you think they can generate elaborate sentence structures, the next moment they are demonstrating extensive signs of anxiety. Moreover, their use of visual and auditory skills are exceptional (Dyslexia Literacy and Clinical Services (SPELD), 2014). Students having a difficult time mastering these patterns demonstrate SFD. Speed and fluency are the greatest struggle for children with SFD. Without the visual cue, these children have a run-on sentence with minimal capitalization and punctuation (Karnik & Karnik, 2012).

As a student begins creating paragraphs, they incorporate the cognitive process of writing. They enter the final stage of dysgraphia, which is PFD.

Paragraph Formation Dysgraphia (PFD)

When it comes to putting more facts and details on paper, students with PFD falter. These children have a very difficult time with the conversational stage of writing. They hate graphic organizers, but many teachers force them to use this type of product to generate essays. The reason they hate graphic organizers is three-fold:

1. They need more space than most of the pre-printed organizers provide.

2. They need much more of a breakdown of the details to create logical paragraphs.

3. They require support for spelling rules, grammar, paragraph transitions, sequencing, and focus. This area of dysgraphia uses more of the cognitive aspects of writing.

These children need your time. Writing their sentences on note cards as they speak their ideas is a great place to start helping them. After the content is on note cards, encourage them to organize the order of the material. Some students will have difficulty with organization and planning. All areas of executive function will impact their ability to write. Understanding compensatory strategies for executive function will benefit this type of dysgraphia. A suggested reading for executive function skills is *Executive Skills in Children and Adolescents: A Practical Guide to Assessment and Intervention* by Peg Dawson and Richard Guare (2010). More treatment ideas and explanation of executive function will be discussed in later chapters.

In summary, children with sentence and paragraph dysgraphia read, copy, and articulate well. They do well using an adult to scribe their sentence first, then they copy it. Their speed and fluency without a visual cue suffer. They need sentence syntax and grammar support. They cannot spell on paper but may excel at spelling orally. They may have difficulty copying from the board, organizing thoughts and materials, and integrating executive functioning skills.

To really understand dysgraphia and if your student has a delay, teachers and parents should also have a basic knowledge of typical reading and writing development, which will be discussed in the next chapter.

Chapter Two

Decoding

ANOTHER TERM FOR breaking material into smaller pieces is decoding. When learning how to read, students break the material down into letters, words, sentences, and paragraphs.

Reading is divided into five main categories: phonemic awareness, phonics, vocabulary development, reading fluency, and reading comprehension. Each of these categories has different subcategories. I am by no means a reading specialist, and the analysis of reading blows my mind, to be frank. Your school district will have a reading specialist on staff. You can also find them in many tutoring organizations such as Sylvan Learning Centers, Huntington Learning Centers, and The Tutor Doctor. There are numerous others. A quick Google search is usually enough to locate specialists in various localities.

Visual perceptual awareness plays a large role in the identification of letters and numbers as symbols and how the symbols are translated to meaning. The meaning of the symbols is translated into sound when read orally. According to Amen and Amen (2017), vision is 50% of our sensory feedback.

Phonemic Awareness

Phonemic awareness is making sense of what is heard. It is the most basic form of communication. A baby and a mother know each other's sounds intuitively. The baby learns to babble and eventually apply syllables to the sounds they imitate from the people around them. They begin to associate objects with those sounds.

Phonics

Once the sounds are associated with meaning, a symbol is used to identify those sounds. Single letter or numeral awareness is part of phonics awareness. Eventually, words are put together and the sounds, or phonics, of the written letters and letter groups are taught. It is in this area that visual perception begins to become an issue if the child cannot put the symbol and sound together. Letters could become mirror images or reversals and frustration begins for the child. At this point, all communication is visual, little writing has begun. However, that does not discount the frustration distinguishing between an "m" and a "w" or a "b" and a "d". If the child has trouble determining letter combinations, continue repeating activities reinforcing phonemic awareness and phonics until phonics is mastered.

Decoding phonics includes reading the letters and numbers. Learning to write letters is encoding and is discussed in the next chapter.

Vocabulary

The third level of development is vocabulary development. This category is divided into listening to letter sounds and vocabulary words, speaking the sounds or words, identifying the letter or reading the vocabulary word. Atypical students require extra time for these pathways to develop. Once the short-term memory of one specific segment of information is recalled easily, fluency will occur.

Reading Fluency

Fourth, reading fluency is the ability to read a series of words in a designated amount of time. Most teachers rely on the child's ability to read orally to track reading fluency. Teachers are typically assessing more skills during a reading assessment than rote fluency. For example, skills such as changing of voice tone to reading with oral expression can be assessed. In addition, students may skip words or lines of text. These skills are related to fluency, but not reading fluency in the purest sense.

Teachers also encounter the child who can memorize and literally repeat verbatim the text. These children are not reading with fluency. They have superior auditory memory. When asked to explain the passage, they cannot.

Children make associations with their personal experiences. These experiences create memory patterns which may help or interfere with reading fluency.

For the child with visual tracking or visual perceptual difficulties, this task could be daunting. Not only does the child need to be able to identify letter and words, they also need to do it within a timed session. These time constraints add internalized pressure for students, hence anxiety. The anxiety can manifest its appearance through behaviors in which fall outside the social norms. These behaviors include, but are not limited to, refusals to complete the task, the fight-flight-fright response, a temper tantrum, or internalized negative self-talk. You may have heard this response called the fight-or-flight response. There is a third option that may occur. When discussing this response, all three terms will be included throughout the book.

In addition, this category requires the child to visually scan the written material from left to right or top to bottom. If the child's eyes are not teaming, or working together, they will have significant problems following along and keeping their place. Adding a finger as a support to pace the reading and to visually track the words can help improve reading fluency. Some signs to look for that indicate vision trouble are squinting, rubbing the eyes, or needing to look at books too close or far away. However, determining a clear diagnosis of visual teaming problems required a complete evaluation by a pediatric optometrist or occupational therapist specializing in visual perception. There is more information on visual tracking and eye teaming in Part Three.

Reading Comprehension

The final area is reading comprehension. This category contains the interpretation of an oral and/or written response to the material that is read. This category encompasses understanding the material that was read, remembering it to answer questions regarding the material, and communicating a response to answer the question provided. When communicating a response, it can be oral or written.

Children who have superior auditory memory and can memorize a passage after hearing it one time, may have a difficult time explaining the passage in their own words. These children have poor reading comprehension.

Some of my colleagues are associated with dyslexia organizations. These organizations use adapted ways of enhancing the reading material through changes in the multi-sensory approach to overcome the dyslexia. Multi-sensory simply means using more than one sense to learn something. More information about sensory learning is included throughout the book.

Chapter Three

Encoding

THE WORD ENCODING has different variations on the same theme in different industries. The computer industry states that encoding is the process of putting a sequence of characters (letters, numbers, punctuation, and symbols) into a specialized format (Rouse, 2005). Genetics states that specific DNA are responsible for producing a substance or behavior. Whereas, the psychological definition of encoding is "any information which we sense and subsequently attempt to process, store, and later retrieve.... breaking the information down into a form we understand" (AlleyDog, n. d.). Psychologists McDermott and Roediger (2018), from Washington University in St. Louis, state that there are three phases to encoded information. The first step is to learn it and relate it to past knowledge. Step two is storing it. Step three is making it accessible to use. Each of these definitions involve taking information and translating it so that it can be used in other formats.

Understanding a process is key to correcting it when it goes wrong. One researcher describes how the parts of the brain encode information:

> Encoding is a biological event beginning with perception through the senses. The process of laying down a memory begins with attention (regulated by the thalamus and the frontal lobes), in which a memorable event causes neurons to fire more frequently, making the experience more intense and increasing the likelihood that the event is encoded as a memory. Emotion tends to increase attention, and the emotional element of an event is processed on an unconscious pathway in the brain leading to the amygdala. Only then are the actual sensations derived from an event processed (Mastin, 2018).

These definitions express the concept of taking information, storing it, and retrieving it to be used as new material.

In contrast to these involved definitions and explanations from neuroscientists, when teachers were asked how they used the term encode, they simply replied, "Spelling."

Educators define decoding as what you read and encoding as what you spell (Bear, Invernizzi, Templeton, & Jonston, 2016). However, there is more involved in encoding than simply spelling. Encoding is a process that your brain uses to neurologically determine how you speak or write.

In the brain, there is a process to produce properly spelled words. For a child to write out a sight word, one piece of the puzzle is their motivation to learn. Dolch (1936) and Fry (1980) have defined high frequency words that are used by many young writers. These words are called sight words.

Like reading, writing is achieved through stages. You must master each stage to master the art of creating a manuscript or essay.

Single Mark Stage: 2 years old

The first time a child holds a crayon in their hand, the marking that occurs on the paper is usually a faint line. It is very short and typically horizontal. The crayon is dropped and off they go to the next activity that catches their attention. This Single

Figure 1 Single Mark Stage

Mark Stage is the first step in teaching their mind how to motor plan what to do when they hold a pencil.

Scribbling Stage: 2 years old

Children begin to take those first markings and begin moving their arm back and forth. Many times, the child is holding some type of crayon. As the child colors, their arm entire arm is moving back and forth. That is the first part of the neural development

Figure 2 Scribbling Stage Mark

process for writing. As the motor planning for the gross motor (larger) muscle groups become integrated, the child will begin to isolate the movements of the fine motor (smaller) muscle groups. Horizontal and vertical scribbles will be the first to emerge followed by circular motions. The circular motions are evidence that the child's arm muscle is learning isolated movement patterns.

Manufacturers have made this stage easier on beginning writers. They have invented crayons today that come in various shapes. One style of crayon is shaped like a bulb with a crayon point on one end. Some other choices for crayons include jumbo and triangular shaped.

Pre-writing Stage: 3 years old

When the child can start and stop writing lines and circles intentionally, this stage has begun. The larger muscle groups of the arm are the flexor muscles, specifically the biceps and muscles on the palm side of your arm. Whereas, the triceps and muscles on the top side of your arm are your extensor muscles. The easiest way to activate these muscles is to show the child how to make lines on paper. Activation is a term used by medical professions that simply means that the muscle is moving or contracting.

The flexor muscles are activated when the crayon is pulled toward the middle of the body. The extensor muscles are activated when the crayon moves away from the body.

As the muscles of your arm become more able to isolate movements, they are ready for more complex challenges. Combining the horizontal and vertical lines to form a cross is the next skill to incorporate. These pre-writing strokes are followed by the circle, then the diagonal top to bottom left to right and right to left. Children who learn to create diagonals from bottom to top may have difficulty with letter formation as writing becomes further established. Once, all these pre-writing strokes are integrated, letter formation can begin.

Figure 3 Pre-Writing Shapes

Letter/Shape Formation: 4-5 years old

After a child has the prewriting skills to form a letter, parents and teachers can begin working with the child to form these lines into letters. Letters associated the cross include, the letters L, F, E, H, T, and I. Because T and I start in the center of the shape, teach them last.

Circular letters are next. They include: C, G, O, and U.

Next, combination letters like D, P, and B can be introduced.

Since, the letters J, R, Q, S, A, K, N, M, V, W, X, Y, Z have more complex features, hold them to last.

Oral language and written language skills develop in virtually opposite Schools need to be aware that programs based on phonics in their English Language Arts programming teach oral letter sounds in an oral language developmental pattern. For example, an "a" is one of the first sounds that we verbalize. Yet, a capital A is one of the most difficult letters to write.

The association between oral and written language begins here. Phonemic awareness and phonics integration of letter formation education should be introduced at this time.

Phonetic Writing: 5-9 years old

As children connect letter sounds with the letter symbol, the phonetic writing emerges. Many times, this stage and pre-primer reading occur simultaneously. Pre-primer is a term associated with first words like cat and dog. It is at this stage that reading children's word formation is difficult because their rudimentary grasp of letter-sound correlation does not always correspond to traditional spelling. For instance, "please" might look like "plez." "Made" is often written "mad". Some other examples are "chrk" for truck or "bunanuz" for bananas.

Emergent phonetic spellers will make copying errors at this stage, even when the sentence is directly above what they are to be copying. Letters are not always spaced adequately apart. Word spacing will emerge by the end of this stage.

As they become more fluent at this stage, the near point copy can move to a paper above the one they are writing on. The last stage of copying from a near point sample, is the copy on the left or right of the child's paper to complete. This style of near point copy will require the child to move their head side to side.

Syllable Development Stage: 5-11 years old

At this stage, children are beginning to create compound words like "sunshine" or "doghouse." They are also moving from writing letters to writing words and sentences.

Midpoint copying is where the student would need to copy from their laptop or from a resource that is two to five feet away. Their head needs to move slightly to obtain the next piece of data.

By age 11, they are expected to write a full page of information. The visual patterns of words and sentence structure are common in their visual memory. By this stage, students should be copying far point information adequately. Far point copying is material that is greater than five feet away. It could be on the board or a poster on the wall. They should also be self-generating their own paragraphs by the end of this writing level.

Conversational Stage: 11-18 years old

The last stage of spelling is where the child integrates the meaning of the writing into the conversation. This advanced stage is not met by everyone. Students who thrive in this stage are creative in their writing. They incorporate imagination and intuition into what they write. Many fictional books are written at this level.

Technical and research-based writing is included in this stage of writing. However, it is more formal and written under specific criterion. Dysgraphia occurs when these developmental milestones develop behind the typical onset of the skill or do not emerge into a student's skill set.

In summary, when you read a book, you are breaking apart the letters and syllables to decode words. When you write the same words on paper, you are encoding them. Difficulty with reading is dyslexia. Difficulty with handwriting is dysgraphia. Difficulty with math concepts is dyscalculia.

In the next part of the book decodes the neural pathways associated with reading and writing. The pathways are simplified for ease of understanding for teachers and parents.

PART TWO

Decoding Neural Pathways

Chapter Four

Neuroscience Introduction

THE BRAIN CONTROLS everything a person does, sees, and hears. This three-pound organ uses 20% of the body's total energy and makes trillions of new cells daily (Taylor, 2016). Repeating the same activity over and over will create a single nerve path. Just like the saying we use when we talk about muscles, "If you don't use it, you lose it." If you do use it, nerves will change into new directions. Our brains can be molded and remolded like play-dough. The concept in neuroscience that explains neural growth is called neuroplasticity.

The early years of a child's life are important to neural growth. Parents may not know typical developmental patterns and milestones. Teachers today are being instructed in early warning signs to identify children with learning disabilities. Overall, educational support is moving forward and taking steps to better address and include all student situations.

Motor Learning Theory states that repetition is how your brain hard wires itself to learn how to make each letter and number (Zwicker & Harris, 2009). Neuroscience is proving again and again that Motor Learning Theory is the key to initial success of any task, including handwriting.

The process of writing is divided into three parts. Handwriting is the mechanical part. This part of the process includes the letter formation, the location a letter is placed on the writing paper, and the neural pathway that is created in the process. Parts two and three are the language and cognitive portions. The language portion of the process is the development of sentence structure. This part contains the grammar, syntax, and basic skills in creating a sentence. The cognitive component is the final portion of handwriting development. It occurs after a child understands the basics of how to write letters and words to create sentences. Once a child can put all three pieces together, the neural pathways of creativity will form paragraphs and essays.

Unlocking a student's potential lies where these parts intersect. By improving the control children have on this intersection point, they can assert more control on their ability to recall the memories around learning. By investing in their memories required to recall letters, spelling words, and other important aspects of learning will exponentially improve. Rote memorization, rote writing, and rote mathematics have been proven to result in some children learning. Incorporating actions with seeing and hearing improves retention.

*Note: Please see your physician for specific diagnoses based on information located in this part of the book. *

Chapter Five

Decoding Brain Anatomy

EVERYTHING THAT HAPPENS in our daily life is controlled by our brain. It controls what we see, hear, touch, taste, smell, feel, and think. To understand a child better, a basic understanding of how the brain and body connections work is necessary. Comprehending the changes from childhood to adulthood will make the process much easier. The following section may seem intense but understanding the biochemical nature of how the brain and body synchronize is important to the topic.

The brain is much more complex than can be explained in one book. To streamline this incredibly involved and multifaceted organ, we will be exploring the major areas.

The brain grows in volume very rapidly during the fetal months and first five years of life. Around five, the brain fills

> Brains that fire together, wire together.
> (Taylor, 2016)

the space provided by the skull. However, the neural network within the brain tissue is constantly changing. This change continues to occur throughout the lifespan and only stops upon death. This concept of continual growth of the brain throughout the lifespan was discovered in 1998 by Eriksson et al.

Prior to that discovery, scientists thought the brain stopped growing in adulthood. The discovery of the changing brain is called neuroplasticity. This research revealed that adults can grow up to 100,000 neural networks every day (Taylor, 2016).

The **central nervous system** is the part of the nervous system that includes the brain and the spinal cord. After the nerves leave the spinal column, the nerves are in the **peripheral nervous system**.

During puberty, a second growth spurt of the body and brain occurs. Brain tissue and nerves form, adding more potential for neural pathway growth. This tissue is in the frontal lobes. As of the time of this printing, scientists believe the frontal lobes becomes fully developed around the age of 25-30 years, although new research may prove that development goes even longer. During each tissue growth period, a person can consciously analyze their environment with more clarity than previously possible. Once the brain is fully developed, it begins to "age." Your brain stops growing tissue around the neural network. However, the neural network continues to create new pathways. This process of developing neural pathways is neuroplasticity.

The best way to protect brain health is to feed it with foods that promote neural communication, and to use it to learn new things.

Dr. Daniel Amen and Dr. Mark Hyman have written several guides, and each have a website with information on which foods promote healthy brain growth. These resources are listed in Appendix A. I am not a nutrition expert; however, I know from experience that when I eat healthier, I feel better. When I follow the plans listed on their websites and in their books, my mental processes work better.

Every day you learn something new, whether you realize that you have learned or not. Psychology research indicates that you create new neural connections with that learning. The harder you work your neural pathways, the longer your brain tissue will remain (Deng, Aimone, & Gage, 2010).

Whether your kids know it or not, they also create these new connections. Neuroscientists have been studying the details of brain structures for many years. To make this organ easier to understand, I am going to divide the brain into four major sections: the brainstem, the cerebellum, the limbic system, and the cortex.

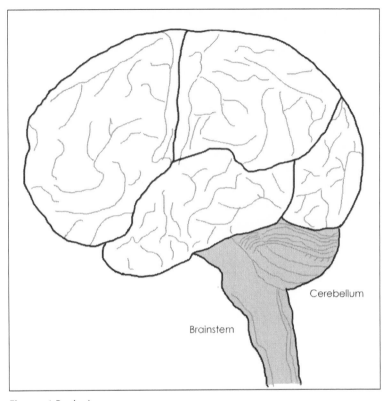

Figure 4 Brainstem

Brainstem

The brainstem is where the automatic responses occur. This part of the brain is in the back of the head where it connects to the neck. It is the oldest part of the brain. The brainstem is also called the reptilian brain because it is most like that of a reptile.

Fetal growth of the brain begins with the brainstem. In the scheme of evolution, the brainstem is present in all cold and warm-blooded animals.

The brainstem controls the parts of the body that automatically excite and calm bodily reactions. The system that controls the functions within the brainstem is called **autonomic nervous system.** The autonomic nervous system controls breathing, body temperature regulation, the urgency to go to the bathroom, and heartbeat. It regulates the parts of our everyday life that we don't even think about. How often do you think about breathing? Most of the day you don't even realize you are breathing. When you are in fight-flight-fright situation, your brain automatically increases your breathing rate, while your breath is shallow when you are relaxed. Have you ever noticed that you don't need to use the bathroom while in fight-or-flight mode? Your brainstem automatically makes the shift using the interaction between these regulatory systems.

To control the opposite responses, the autonomic nervous system needs a way to turn on and shut off a response. These alternating responses are completed by the sympathetic and parasympathetic nervous systems. Think of it this way: the pathway that excites your body's response to what is happening around you is the **sympathetic nervous system** and the system that calms the body down is the **parasympathetic nervous system.** Metaphorically, the sympathetic nervous system is the crisis or triage unit and the parasympathetic nervous system is in control when you are sitting on the beach. The sympathetic nervous system assists in activating the body responses to the fight-flight-fright response. It increases your breathing and heart rates, gets your muscles ready for action, and constricts body functions like digestion and constricts blood flow. Whereas, the parasympathetic nervous system relaxes the body and heart rate (MedicineNet, Definition of autonomic nervous system, 2016).

Take a moment. Take a deep breath. Breathe in to the count of three, as you breathe out, count to six.

By thinking about breathing, you just bypassed the brainstem and made breathing a conscious activity. Other parts of the brain influenced the brainstem. You will learn how this works later. For now, when we are not thinking of our breathing, it is automatically controlled by our brainstem. When it shifts to a conscious control, our breathing mechanism becomes what I call Conscious Breathing. I have heard this type of breathing called Buddha or Yoga breathing. I have chosen Conscious Breathing because you need to intentionally think about breathing.

Let's summarize the brain stem:

- It's the oldest part of the brain.

- It is at the base of the brain.

- It controls the automatic responses of our body.

- It can be overridden by other parts of the brain.

A symptom that indicates there is a problem in the brainstem can be a simple as difficulty regulating bodily functions. One disruption of bodily functions that can occur with children is difficulty sleeping. Another area could be the regulation of body temperature.

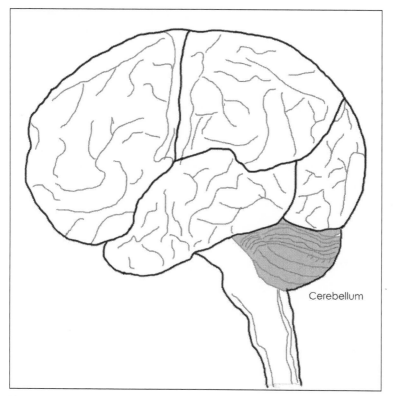

Figure 5 Cerebellum

Cerebellum

The cerebellum is part of the brainstem. It is the largest "organ" in the brain. The cerebellum is the refinement center, meaning it takes every movement we make and smooths it out, eliminating jerky movements. The cerebellum also assists the hippocampus and basal ganglia in the limbic system, to remember and execute refined movements. The cerebellum is used heavily by babies who are learning to transition to becoming toddlers as they learn to walk. Here, movement becomes the normal patterns we see.

The cerebellum also interacts with all other areas of the brain. It assists the cortex to interpret sensory input to create purposeful motor output.

Developmental delays of the cerebellum may display themselves as clumsiness in a child. The child who is always falling all over themselves may have difficulty with the neural connections leading to and from the cerebellum.

For example, children with dysgraphia may have difficulty with smooth lines when writing: jerky pencil marks that result in frustration and refusal to write. These movements may be a result of cerebellar pathway dysfunction. For more information on the clumsy child, please refer to a book on Sensory Processing Disorder (SPD), such as the resources listed in Appendix B.

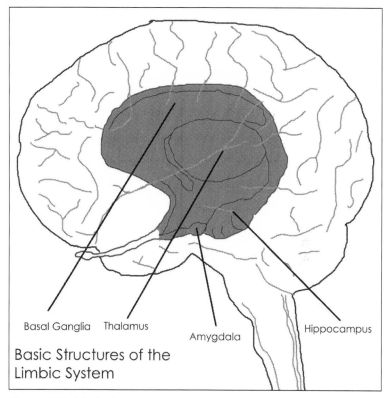

Basal Ganglia   Thalamus

Amygdala

Hippocampus

Basic Structures of the
Limbic System

Figure 6 Limbic System

Limbic System

As you move from the brainstem, the next section you encounter is the limbic system. The **limbic system** is in the center of the brain. It controls our emotions, short-term memory, and codes our movements into a file like a computer program. Each movement becomes associated with our emotions. That's why you recall hitting a baseball after becoming proficient at the task. As our heart is in the center of our chest, the limbic system is in the center of our brain and is often referred to as our emotional heart.

There are four components of the limbic system that we will be discussing in this chapter: the amygdala, hippocampus, the basal ganglia, and the thalamus.

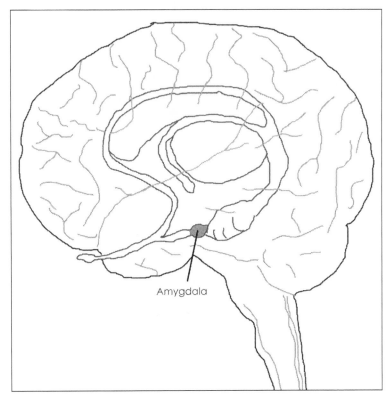

Amygdala

Figure 7 Amygdala

Amygdala

The amygdala is the fear center. It controls how the brainstem responses to the fight-flight-fright response. It is located just above the brainstem in the center of the brain. It relays messages down to the brainstem, but also to the hippocampus and other parts of the brain.

The amygdala helps the autonomic nervous system regulate the sympathetic and parasympathetic systems. If you are in a situation that tells your brain there is danger, the sympathetic nervous system will increase your heart rate, shut down your non-essential body functions, and excrete cortisol. Cortisol is the hormone that is released when you are under stress. The amygdala also releases cortisol in situations of excitement. The brain cannot tell the difference between excitement and a negative experience. It is the memory attached to the response of the experience that becomes a short-term memory and later a long-term memory.

Cortisol is not always a bad thing. It has its place. However, if a person has too many bad experiences happening around them, too much cortisol can overwhelm the system. All hormones in moderation!

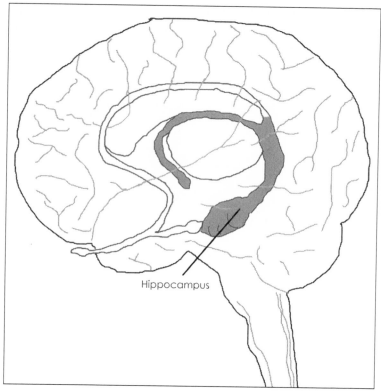

Hippocampus

Figure 8 Hippocampus

Hippocampus

The hippocampus is the short-term memory center. It is a seahorse shaped organ that sits along the amygdala. It has a right and left hemispheric portion. All good and bad memories flow through this location. The hippocampus links our memory with an emotion which are generated in the amygdala.

The hippocampus takes what is happening throughout the day and stores it in files. We have files that happened within the last few minutes and files that occurred this morning. For us to recall them, the hippocampus must keep them in "working" order to access them. This quick access file is our **working memory**. The hippocampus keeps our daily memories in segmented files by time until we sleep. Each memory is linked to an emotion. During sleep, the memories leave the hippocampus and are filed in the long-term memory center. Before we move onto the thalamus, let's look at the impact of the hippocampus during sleep.

Figure 9 Sleep

When you sleep, the short-term memories in the hippocampus are converted to long-term memories. Each one is stored in another section of the brain. When you need to recall them, they emerge back in the hippocampus and working memory area of the brain.

Sleep encompasses a four-step cycle that is repeated throughout the night. Three non-rapid eye movement (NREM) stages, and one rapid eye movement (REM) stage, complete a cycle. The entire cycle including all four stages lasts about 90 minutes to two hours. It is during REM sleep that researchers have found that the working memory is moved to long term memory in the temporal lobes.

People that have trouble sleeping may never get to REM sleep, and therefore never move the daily memory bank to long term memory. As a result, they have two days' worth of data to process through to retrieve necessary information. When the hippocampus has too much information in storage, it becomes overwhelmed and cannot properly access the information. When this occurs, the other part of your limbic system, the basal ganglia, gets the wrong information and unacceptable social behaviors occur. The amygdala activates the fight-flight-fright response. Most humans will over-react or shutdown to situations that occur in a sleep deprived state. When we are calm and rested, we are clear in our focus and attention.

I have a student that I am treating right now; let's call him GG. He had a stroke around two years of age. His little mind runs at the speed of a freight train without brakes, and I often need to remind him to stop and he needs to do it my way occasionally. He was like that when I saw him recently. I turned on some classical music and he immediately calmed down and listened to my interaction with him. Before he calmed down, GG's amygdala was sending responses to his brain and his hippocampus was recalling memories of the past in which his brain said, "Handwriting is a threat. Stay away." His fight-flight-fright response was confusing the old memories with new ones. For instance, his brain could have been saying:

- Fight – He was fighting me to complete a hand-writing task.

- Flight – Avoidance is the amygdala and the hippo-campus recalling memories of "It's too hard." "That caused you pain before." "Run for the hills, baby."

- Fright – He could have demonstrated an emo-tional outburst that would have had the others in the home running (he is cyber-schooled).

With the music playing, he sat right down and began writing. It was beautiful! I had never seen this before from him. With some trials over a few weeks, his mom and I discovered that the music provided focus and improved his productivity in all subjects of the school curriculum.

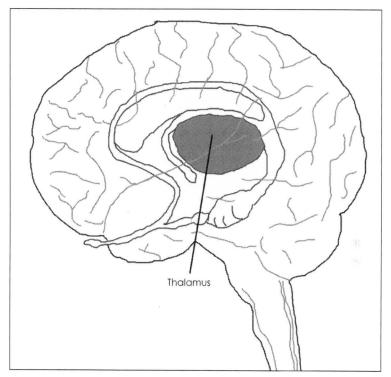

Figure 10 Thalamus

Thalamus

The thalamus resides on top of the brainstem. The interpretation of thalamus from the Greek origin is "chamber". It connects the brainstem and limbic system and is the gatekeeper of the limbic system. It filters the sensory system from all peripheral sensory systems. These systems are defined in chapter six. One major role of the thalamus is to control whether a person is awake or asleep. Second, it filters visual stimuli to the occipital lobes. Third, it regulates auditory information that is sent to the auditory cortex. Finally, it coordinates motor control, coordination, and modulates the intensity of movements and motor planning. More details on motor control are included in chapter seven. Information is sent to many areas of the cerebellum and cortex. This information allows the brain to associate individual pieces of information with other pieces of data and allows the brain to funnel the data into one message that is sent to the basal ganglia (Purves, et al., 2012).

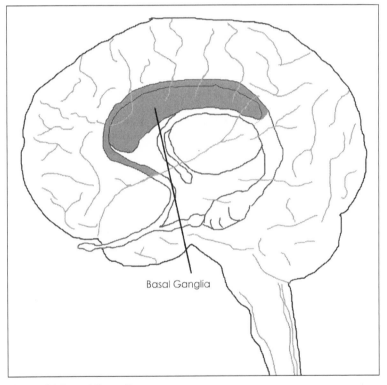

Figure 11 Basal Ganglia

Basal Ganglia

The basal ganglia are groups of tissue masses near the hippocampus that take our movement patterns and support the hippocampus and the amygdala to convert movement from short-term memory and move them to long term memory. The basal ganglia control the movement that occurs because of processing all the information.

The basal ganglia tell us what to do with the information that is processed. Much research has been done on the basal ganglia in the last twenty years. It converts cognitive information from the cortex, refined movements from the cerebellum, and emotional and memory connections of the limbic systems, and relays it to the body. The neural pathways do all this communication in a millisecond.

In my story of my student, did you note how quickly he stopped his fight response? It was almost instantaneous! It is so exciting to see the response to how the limbic system takes a negative reaction and converted it to a positive response!

As he picks up the pencil, the limbic system sends messages everywhere in the brain, receives details back, and sends a message through the basal ganglia to the nerves and muscles to pick up the pencil. Just think of when that does not work smoothly. You may see reactions like tremors, or jerky behaviors.

If you have a child with tremors, please see your doctor. He or she may refer you to an occupational therapist for adaptive ideas and products to reduce the tremors for handwriting.

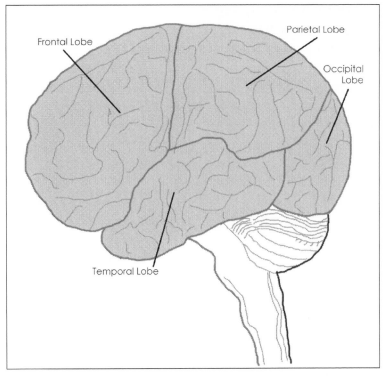

Figure 12 Cortex

Cortex (Neocortex or Cerebrum)

Lastly, we have the cortex, the control center. This part of the brain is also called the neocortex or cerebrum. The cortex is what sets humanity apart from other species. It is the most refined part of the brain, and where conscious thought comes from. The cortex can override the lower parts of the brain if we "think" it through. The cortex is separated into different lobes that each have a right and left side. The lobes are called the occipital, temporal, parietal, and frontal lobes. The view shown in the diagram is looking at the brain from the left side of the head.

When we were talking about conscious breathing earlier, it is the cortex that takes over the control of the brainstem to alter your breathing patterns. The cortex relays messages to the basal ganglia and down through the brainstem to the body. Brainstem breathing takes back control when you are not thinking about your breathing patterns.

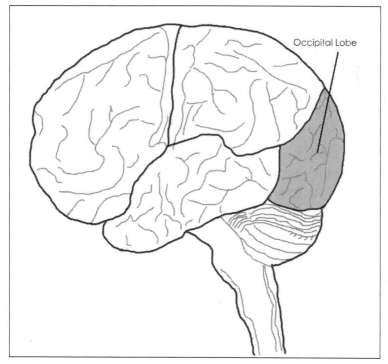

Figure 13 Occipital Lobe

Occipital Lobes

The occipital lobes take what we see in our retina and coverts it to color forms and determines the motion of an object that we see. It is in the occipital lobes that form, shape, and the direction of that motion are detected. The information received by the retina is upside down and travels the optic nerve to disperse images from both eyes into both occipital lobes.

This information is shared with all other areas of the brain and interpreted. According to Dr. Daniel Amen (2017), "50% of your brain is dedicated to vision." Your occipital lobes are quite important when it comes to interpreting what we see. The nerves that travel from the retina to the occipital lobes pass through the limbic system before arriving in the occipital lobes. Each object we see is documented in our brain with an emotion and short-term memory. After interpretation, what we saw gets converted to a long-term memory while we sleep. Each visual is interpreted for the emotions attached with it and is stored in the hippocampus. It is the occipital lobes that originally analyze all the colors, forms, and movements associated with that memory.

The occipital lobes take the "digital" information from the eyes and translate it to color, form, shape, and motion. The information is divided and sent to the temporal, parietal, and frontal lobes for interpretation. Alterations in the way we interpret information are called illusions. Don't always believe what you think you see. Let's look at this drawing. Remember, the occipital lobes only create the digital code for what is seen. The other lobes do the interpretation. How many faces do you see?

You should see ten.

Figure 14 Tree of Leaders

Figure 15 Tree of Leaders Answers

This illustration is known as "*The National Leaders Tree*". It was "drawn in the 1880's by an unnamed illustrator for Harper's Illustrated. It has been variously claimed to represent Indian leaders, South American leaders, and Russian leaders. It originally was meant to illustrate British leaders (BrainPages, 2018).

The interpretations of colors, forms, and shapes that are registered in the occipital lobes are sent to the temporal and parietal lobes. Movements are sent to be interpreted in the cerebellum, pre-frontal cortex, and basal ganglia (Purves, et al., 2012).

The occipital lobes cannot tell you that the red, mostly-round object that was just tossed to you is an apple. It can only describe the apple as red, mostly-round, and that it is moving toward you.

Once the red, mostly-round object is analyzed for color and shape, it is the other areas of the cortex that tell our memory what it is. It is only after our memory and emotions recognize it as an apple that our mouth begins to salivate. If our movement response is not accurate and precise, we won't catch it.

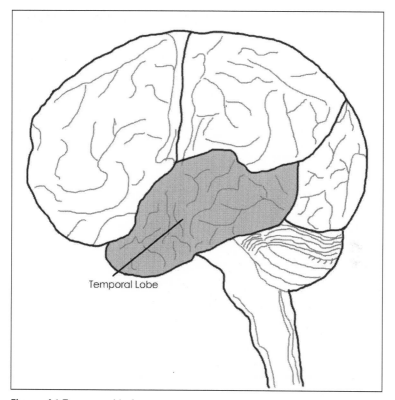

Temporal Lobe

Figure 16 Temporal Lobe

Temporal Lobes

As we move to the sides of the brain just behind your ears, we come to the temporal lobes. Remember that I told you the hippocampus stores the short-term or working memory and mixes it with the emotions in the amygdala? After we sleep and move through all the sleep cycles, the memories move to the temporal lobes. The temporal lobes are where long-term memory is stored.

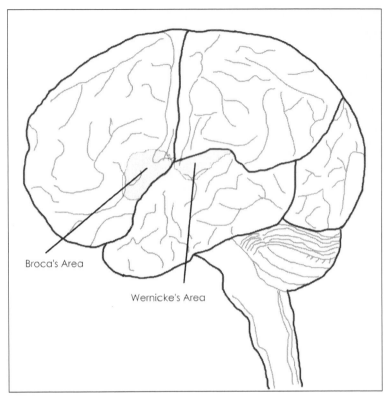

Figure 17 Broca's and Wernicke's Area

In addition to long term memory, the temporal lobes also contain the centers necessary to translate what we hear. Our ears take the sound waves of our environment and change them into digital patterns. These patterns move to a portion of the temporal lobes that takes what we hear and receives it. This area is called the **Wernicke's area.** Wernicke's area is known for receptive language. From this area, the messages are sent to the limbic system and other parts of the cortex for interpretation. The messages bounce back to the temporal lobes to the **Broca's area** (expressive language) before making the last trip through the basal ganglia and down through the brain stem to make a movement. It is very important to understand that we receive messages at a different location of the temporal lobes than we express them.

These expressions can be oral or written. After being interpreted in Broca's area, oral language and written language are further processed in different areas of the brain. This results in different types of expressive language. Because of these different neural pathways, oral or written language-based difficulties could occur. These include oral dyspraxia or dysgraphia, respectively.

Receptive and expressive language are the foundation of reading and writing. Difficulties in these areas are worked on by several related services providers. Speech and language pathologists (SLP), vision therapists, and occupational therapists could be some of the professionals that help a child with language difficulties.

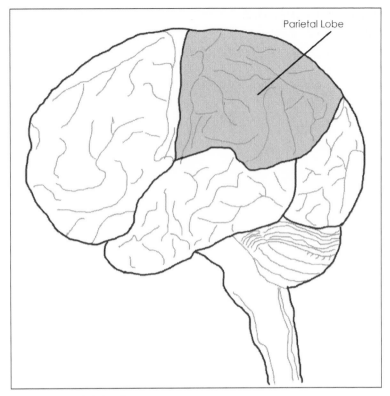

Figure 18 Parietal Lobe

Parietal Lobes

The parietal lobes do all the interpreting from our vision and hearing. This area coordinates all our visual and auditory perceptions. Once all the parts of our vision and hearing are interpreted, the part of the parietal lobes called the **motor cortex** contacts the frontal lobes for final instructions, then tell the basal ganglia what messages to send to the body. When this area of the brain does not work efficiently, many tasks that we take for granted don't work well. For example, this area of the brain helps us feed ourselves independently. It also helps us bathe, dress, and move about our environment effectively. Additionally, if this area of the brain is not working properly, a person's handwriting will be a source of anguish and the amygdala will try to override rational thoughts and send messages to the hippocampus that, "Writing is evil. Don't do it." Rationally, we know that is a false thought, but kids can't combat what they are feeling at such a young age since their frontal lobes are not finished growing.

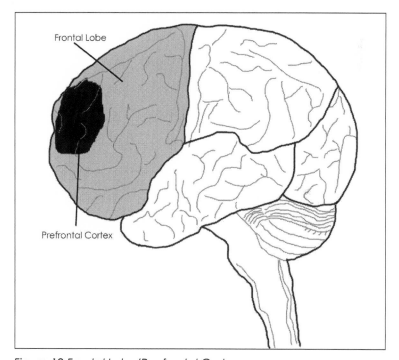

Figure 19 Frontal Lobe/Pre-frontal Cortex

Frontal Lobes

The last area of the cortex is the **frontal lobes**. The frontal lobes are like the Chief Executive Officer (CEO) of the brain. The part of the frontal lobes called the **pre-frontal cortex (PFC)**, is the home of the final decision-making organ of the brain and our executive functioning skills. The PFC is essentially the last ascending (sensory) destination of a message from the body. It determines how the rest of the brain will respond if given the opportunity. However, if the person reacts to a situation by instinct, the PFC never gets the message.

The frontal lobes of elementary students are small and do not come to maturation until after puberty. This is the part of the brain that grows from ages 10-12 to about 25 years (some researchers are even saying up to 35 years) (Taylor, 2016). Because the brain is not fully developed, children need extra help and patience for most new experiences. Not just the elementary student learning basic skills, but also the high school senior filling out paperwork to enter college. Even adults learning new tasks work better with a coach to learn new tasks.

When you are learning a new task, it takes 20% more energy than after you have developed a neural pathway for the task (Taylor, 2016). After it is learned, and our brains have created the neural pathway to complete the task, it is automated in our brains. As mentioned earlier however, if you don't continue to use it, your brain will override it and create a new pathway to automate something else.

The pre-frontal cortex helps us execute several higher-level activities including, but not limited to, the areas identified in the **executive function.** Peg Dawson and Richard Guare discuss their research on executive function in full in the book, *Executive Skills in Children and Adolescents: A Practical Guide to Assessment and Intervention, Second Edition* (2010). This image was created based on their work.

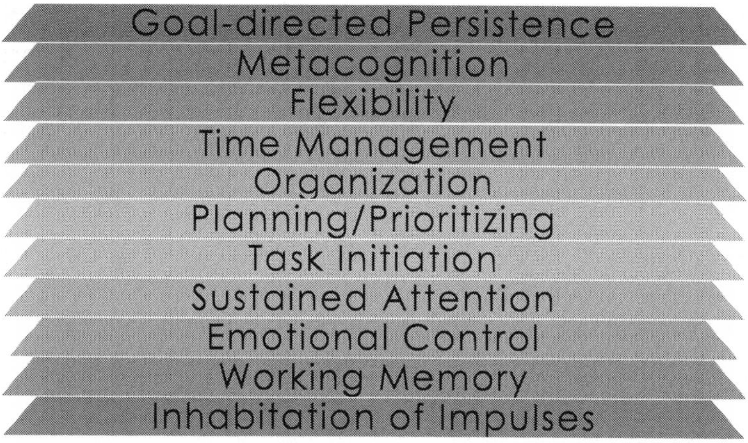

| Goal-directed Persistence |
| Metacognition |
| Flexibility |
| Time Management |
| Organization |
| Planning/Prioritizing |
| Task Initiation |
| Sustained Attention |
| Emotional Control |
| Working Memory |
| Inhabitation of Impulses |

Figure 20 Executive Function (Dawson & Guare, 2010)

According to their work, the bottom of the image makes up the more basic executive functions. Infants begin developing behavioral inhibition to impulses, non-verbal working memory, and emotional control at about 5 months. Verbal working memory and speech develop around 2-3 years of age. Planning and prioritizing and the remaining executive functions emerge around 6 years of age but are not fully developed until well into young adulthood.

However, if you are in a fight-flight-fright situation, even inhibiting impulses may be overridden by the limbic system. You will need to consciously think about controlling these executive functions in new learning or stressful situations. However, the frontal lobe's job is to overrule all other parts of the brain and its functions. Elite military personnel have learned how to keep the PFC from being overridden by the limbic system.

Attention Deficit Hyperactivity Disorder (ADHD) causes chronic disease processes which in turn cause unusual behaviors in children and adults. Traumatic Brain Injuries (TBIs) and concussions may cause damage to the frontal lobes and other parts of the brain. However, the frontal lobes are the most common victim. Diseases and injuries such as these significantly impact the function of the frontal lobes. Intellectual Quotient (IQ) testing is primarily examining develop-ment of the executive functioning skills if the individual. Students with diagnoses such as these generally score below the normal range on IQ tests. This score signifies a learning disability. With diagnoses such as ADHD or a TBI, students may exhibit symptoms such as:

- Not understanding facial expressions.
- Difficulty expressing oneself.
- Thinking concretely and have difficulty with abstract information.
- Difficulty inferring an answer.
- Having fewer words in their vocabulary.

All information from this part of the brain is sent back through the basal ganglia before heading down to the peripheral nervous system.

Left and Right Hemispheres

When looking at the brain from front to back, there is a distinct divide down the center forming the left and right hemispheres. Generally, what happens on the left side of the body is stored in the right hemisphere and what happens of the right side of the body is stored in the left hemisphere (Purves, et al., 2012). Research has noted that the left side of the brain is more analytical and logical. Whereas, the right brain is creative and imaginative (Purves, et al., 2012).

In the early days of life, a child is exploring his/her world. The neural pathways of exploration are expressed through the neural pathways on the right hemisphere. One can build up the right hemisphere by using music, art, and movement. Daydreaming, humming, creative writing, and storytelling are strong activators of neural pathways on the right side of one's brain.

Entering kindergarten requires students to begin strengthening the left side, which is the logical side of one's brain. Emergent reading skills and early writing use much of students' cortices as they master the tasks. Some children have difficulty making this shift in neural development. These difficulties could be demonstrated by zoning out and daydreaming or singing or humming to themselves. The neural pathways resort to completed, comfortable pathways to avoid the work of forging new ones. These students may appear reluctant to learn, but don't fall for that myth. Children usually want to meet the expectations of the adults in their lives.

Be reassured that their behavior is simply a result of neural pathways that are still under construction. The pathways needed a short break from building. A movement break is a good way to reboot the brain. The movement gives it a chance to refuel. Adding a song or storytelling moment will also provide the needed brain distraction.

These children have a strong intuition. Intuition is that small voice or butterflies in the stomach that tells you when something is okay or not right. Most adults have learned this response as the stress response and take heed to its warning, while others do not. Children do not have the cognitive capacity to really understand what they are feeling. Social skills and role modeling will help students better understand these feelings.

The strong intuition that is created by the imagination of the right hemisphere can be mistaken for perfectionism. These students know when something does not look perfect. They tend to erase their work and redo it until frustration shuts them down. The student feels like they cannot meet the expectations of the adult.

In summary, the brain controls your every movement, thought, and behavior. The brainstem controls your basic needs like temperature regulation and heart rate. A special portion of the brainstem, the cerebellum, refines your movements and eliminates the potential for jerkiness. The limbic system controls your fear response. However, your cortex can regain control over these portions of the brain by training yourself to respond differently. The cognitive portions of your brain analyze the sensory input and give the body feedback through a motor response. These cognitive portions include the occipital, parietal, temporal, and frontal lobes. After decisions are made in the brain, messages travel along the sensory pathways to the body.

Chapter Six

Sensory: The Decoding Pathway

KEEPING THE PROCESS simple, you first have a stimulus from the environment such as the wind passing by your arm. Next, your nervous system reacts to it and a change occurs in your brain. The hair on your skin moves which stimulates the nerve follicle to send a message to the brain. Finally, some sort of motor output occurs. It could be refreshing on a hot summer day or a chill on a cool day. The output could be motor, behavioral, or information storage. Steps one, two, and three are the sensory portion. Step four is the motor response. Motor pathways are discussed in the next chapter.

Sensory-Motor Pathway

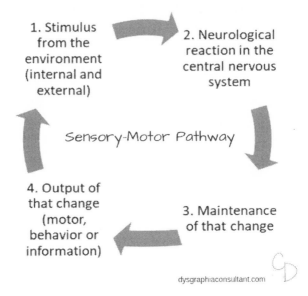

Figure 21 Sensory-Motor Pathway

Every sensation that we taste, smell, touch, hear, and see follows its own neural pathway from the site of the sensation through the body, through the brain, and back to the site of the sensation. These pathways are called sensory-motor pathways. In addition to the traditional five senses, we have several other neural pathways in our sensory-motor system.

To understand how handwriting and the brain work, we need to explore what is going on from a sensory-motor perspective. A sensory response is anything and everything that meets your body that sends a message to your brain about what is happening in the environment around you. That includes everything you see, hear, touch, taste, and smell. When you were in grade school, your teacher told you that you have five senses: vision, hearing, smell, taste, and touch. They gave you a partial truth; you have ten neural sensory pathways. These neural sensory pathways are specific neural groups that use basic neural sensory-motor groups to complete the pathway. They do not include the basic regulatory systems used by the sympathetic and parasympathetic nervous systems to regulate body functions. The ones that you know are examined in the tables below:

Table 1 Common Sensory Systems

Visual	Seeing	Color features are seen on the retina
Auditory	Hearing	Sound waves are intercepted with sound receptors in the ear
Olfactory	Smell	Odors interact with smell receptors in nose
Gustatory	Taste	Flavors interact with taste receptors (taste buds) on tongue
Tactile	Touch	• *Light Touch* – like hair touching skin • *Deep Pressure* – pressure increase/ decrease that is placed on joints • *Pain (nociceptors)* – response to noxious stimuli • *Temperature (thermoreceptors)* – sense the heat or coldness of an object • *Protective Sensation* -Protects from dangers injuring skin such as a deep cut through multiple layers of skin

Each sensory system contains its own neural pathway. For instance, vision begins in the retina of the eye and follows a specific path through the brain and coordinates with all other systems to create a mental image of what the person sees and a corresponding response or movement. For example, handwriting coordinates what is seen by the eye with the movement of using the hand to write. The sensory portion is what is seen. The motor portion is the movement. All systems respond in this manner.

As you can see in the table, touch encompasses much more than just touching the skin. There are five tactile pathways that monitor your environment: light touch, deep pressure, pain, temperature, and protective sensation.

The areas of vision, hearing, smell, and taste are more straightforward with respect to the sensation information you learned in school. However, each sensation is very complex in the nerve pathways that are used to make it from the point of origin to your brain.

The additional five senses that were alluded to earlier include the proprioception, vestibular, kinesthetic, stereognosis, and graphesthesia systems.

Proprioception

The first term, proprioception, is used often when discussing sensory processing. Pushing a joint together makes it compress. When it is released, it stretches. This cycle of compression and release is called proprioception. It is the sense of deep pressure inside the joint that keeps it stable, so your muscles and bones can work together (Norkin & Levangie, 1992). Your body interprets where it is in space based on the neural feedback provided by the compression of the joint.

When you push down on your knee when you are doing a jumping jack, your ligaments and tendons around the joint push it together. When you release contact with the ground, the ligaments and tendons stretch to lengthen your knee joint. This occurs in every joint in your body. This process also occurs when a child is using their fingers to hold a pencil. The joints in the fingers trigger nerves to cause the muscles and bones to stabilize around the pencil to begin writing. A. Jean Ayres coined this term in the late 1970's. She states that the term originates from the Latin word for "one's own." "Sensations from the muscles and joints...tell the brain when and how the muscles are contracting or stretching, and when and how the joints are bending, extending, or being pulled or compressed" (Ayers, 1979, p. 183). Over time, occupational therapists have refined the definition. Pedretti (1990) states that proprioception "refers to unconscious information about joint position and movement that arises from receptors in the muscles, joints, ligaments, and bone." Again, a specific tactile neural sensory path is responsible for each proprioception reaction.

Vestibular System

The vestibular system has more of a neurological web to its connections, which makes it more complicated. A simple explanation of the vestibular system is that it tells the body how fast and in what direction your head is moving (Pedretti, 1990). It uses feedback from the proprioceptive system in the joints, your vision, and your head and neck movements to tell you where you are according to the environment. The three main vestibular reflexes are listed in the table. It is called **Hidden Sensory Pathways** and is located at the end of this chapter.

The vestibular ocular reflex, the vestibular spinal reflex, and the vestibular colic reflex tell the brain where your head is going and how fast is it moving in a specific direction. You could be sitting at your desk, in a car, or on a roller coaster. This is the system that can make you get sick if you have had too much movement (Hain & Helminski, 2007). The messages from the vestibular system are sent to the brain through the brainstem, cerebellum, limbic system, and cortices make the executive decision how to move from this information.

An intact vestibular system helps children copy from the board. If parts of this complex system are working inefficiently, the child may exhibit any number of symptoms. First, they could get dizzy or light-headed when copying from the board. Second, they could have difficulty sitting still at their desk. Third, they could have difficulty playing outside on playground equipment. This system impacts more than these few examples. See the **Hidden Sensory Pathway** table at the end of the chapter.

Kinesthesia

Third, kinesthesia gives the brain feedback to tell how far we should move. Have you ever played soccer? Knowing how far to jump to hit the ball with your chest is one example of this internal sensation. This sense is defined as the "conscious awareness of joint position and movement," or where your body is in relation to its environment (Pedretti, 1990). Try envisioning yourself attempting to copy a sentence from the blackboard to a designated location on paper. Your head must look at the board, then the paper, and repeat the alternative postures to complete the sentence. Now, try to repeat this task with your eyes closed. Your brain learns how far to move your head. Open your eyes after several repetitions. Are you looking at the blackboard or paper? See the **Hidden Sensory Pathway** table at the end of the chapter.

Stereognosis

Stereognosis is the ability to identify common objects without vision (Pedretti, 1990, p. 187). Have you ever put you hand in your pocket and tried to find your keys among change, paper clips, pens, and anything else that may end up in your pocket? Your ability to find your keys is stereognosis. This sense combines the neural tactile pathways to identify an object. Depending on the material or object that you are looking for with your fingers, you could use all five sensory pathways. See the **Hidden Sensory Pathway** table at the end of the chapter.

Graphesthesia

Finally, graphesthesia is the ability to recognize symbols and shapes such as letters and numbers that are written on the skin without seeing what was written (Pedretti, 1990, p. 189). This sensation is used when you make letters or numbers on someone else's back and they try to guess what you wrote. This sensation can be done anywhere on the skin. Graphesthesia creates a neural pathway linking light touch and proprioception

In short, these sensations are important in feeding information to the brain about which way the body is moving and how quickly. Their information gets combined with the vestibular and kinesthetic feedback to help the brain tell the body what to do next. See the **Hidden Sensory Pathway** table at the end of the chapter.

Table 2 Hidden Sensory Pathway

Proprioception	Deep pressure	• Located in the joints • Tells the brain how much pressure is on the body • Static-no movement • Dynamic – movement is occurring • Tells brain where the body parts are and what they are doing • Compression, stretch, vibration • Mobility and stability
Vestibular	Movement	• Related to the movement of the body part • How much movement is the body part going to need to move to perform the task • 3-part system interlocking vision, proprioception, and central nervous system • Sense of movement and balance with relation to the head and body in the physical environment
Kinesthesia	Telling Distance without vision	• The ability to tell where a body part or an object is without looking at it
Stereognosis	Feeling without seeing	• The ability to identify an object without seeing it • Example: finding your keys in your pocket
Graphesthesia	Identifying symbols without vision	• The ability to identify symbols on the body without seeing what is written • Example: telling a number or letter written on back

An example that I have used to describe the difference between proprioceptive, vestibular, and the kinesthetic sense is driving a car. The amount of pressure that you need to push the brake to stop and the accelerator to move is proprioception. The proprioception tells the joint how much deep pressure it needs to push on the pedal. Although your head remains essentially stationary, or static, when you are moving; once you brake, your head moves. The change in velocity of the car activates the vestibular system so that your body adjusts to the change in car speed. You will notice that your head will bobble a few times; that is the lag in motor response to the vestibular input. The movement that your leg and foot make to change position from the accelerator to the brake is done without vision. However, the driver knows exactly how far to move the lower limb. This sensation of knowing how far to move your limb is the kinesthetic sense. Finding a cup under your seat while driving uses all the hidden senses to identify the cup without looking.

Now, think of when someone else is driving and you are paying attention to the road. If you also know how to drive, how often does your foot instinctively go for the pedal before you feel the person driving do so? Do you feel your joints tense and brace yourself? Do you feel your neck muscle tighten? Do you feel the need to look away? Those responses are your hidden senses assessing the environment and alerting your body for the change.

Handwriting Connection

In summary, these hidden senses are used throughout the handwriting process. First, proprioception is used to apply pressure to a pencil to write and to keep your body in an upright position at the desk. Second, your vestibular system moves your head around to see the blackboard or paper. Third, kinesthesia is used when a student writes his name with his eyes closed. It is especially used during cursive writing to create the flow of connected letters in a word. Fourth, students use stereognosis to find crayons or a glue stick in their pencil box while talking to their neighbor. Finally, graphesthesia is used to identify kind versus aggressive touches from other students.

Chapter Seven

Encoding: The Motor Pathway

ALL SENSORY INPUT is followed by a **motor response**. That response can be a physical reaction, mental redirection of information, or a behavioral response. Messages leave the basal ganglia and target where the appropriate location in the body that needs to respond. Motor responses of the neuromuscular system are isolated in four categories **(CAPS)**:

Control
Accuracy
Precision
Speed

When looking at the physical reaction to a sensory response, sensory integrative theory states that the developmental milestones are accomplished through a systematic hierarchical process. There are four core requirements for a controlled motor response to function well. The response should be accurate, precise, well-controlled, and have appropriate speed for the smooth movement to happen.

Control

An infant utilizes tactile, proprioceptive, and vestibular sensory stimuli to develop postural control. According to Pollock, Durward, Rowe, & Paul (2000), "**postural control** is defined as the act of maintaining, achieving or restoring a state of balance during any posture or activity." According to Fischman (2007), head and neck are developed first, followed by prone extension (holding head up while on hands and knees), then sitting, standing, and finally walking. Students must freely move from these gross motor postures to make fine motor activities manageable.

One of the first gross motor movements that the brain-body connect is the location of the head in relation to the body. There is a series of neural pathways that tells the brain the position of the head with respect to the neck and rest of the body. To hold your head upright, it must be stable on your neck. **Stability** within the neuromuscular system is the "ability to control the center of mass relative to the base of support" (Fischman, 2007). Proper posture for handwriting is to have feet, ankles, and hips at 90° angles with back erect, but slightly forward. Elbows should be resting on the table. Arms will rest at an approximate 45° angle from their sides. **Motor control** is "how the neuromuscular system functions to activate and coordinate the muscles and limbs involved in the performance of motor skills, both new skills, and those already acquired" (Fischman, 2007). Motor control is separated into large and small muscle groups. Large muscle groups yield gross motor movements like kicking a ball or hitting a ball with a bat, whereas fine motor control is dictated by small muscles groups like the fingers. Handwriting is controlled by a combination of gross and small muscle groups throughout the arm and body. Neuromuscular control of the entire body is called postural control.

Postural control and coordination of movements of the hand is called eye-hand coordination, or if the foot is involved, eye-foot coordination. **Eye-hand (or foot) coordination** is the ability of the vision system to coordinate the information received through the eyes (feet) to control, guide, and direct the hands in the accomplishment of a given task (Laberge, 2015).

My daughter is a physics major, so I asked her about concepts in physics that can be applied to the body. The concepts in simple machines can be used to help us understand postural control or eye-hand (or foot) coordination. The movement of the elbow is a lever. A lever is a simple machine.

Accuracy and Precision

Accuracy and precision begin developing once muscular control is established. To parents, postural control, accuracy, and precision appear to develop at the same time. Whether we like it or not, Newton's laws apply to everyday body movements. According to the laws of physics, **accuracy** refers to how close the measured value is to the true or accepted value and **precision** refers to how close together a group of measurements are to each other.

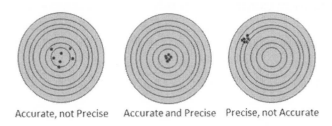

Accurate, not Precise   Accurate and Precise   Precise, not Accurate

Figure 22 Accuracy and Precision (Roll2Roll Technologies, Inc., 2017)

Precision has nothing to do with the true or accepted value of a measurement, so it is quite possible to be very precise and totally inaccurate.

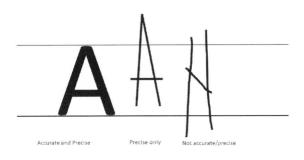

Accurate and Precise   Precise only   Not accurate/precise

Figure 23 Accuracy and Precision Letter A

You can see in the first drawing of the letter A. It is accurate and precise. The second drawing looks like a floating A; the cross bar is over shot, but the precise placement of the line relative to one another make the figure easily recognizable as an A. The third drawing depicts what appears to be more of the letter H instead of the letter A. This A lacks precision in the not-touching diagonal strokes and the diagonal placement of the crossbar: it's the wrong shape. However, the vertical rather than diagonal lines which form the sides of the A are also inaccurate, since the placement of the top of the strokes is far from where they belong. It is also inaccurately using the three-lined paper, extending above and below the accepted placement.

Speed and Fluency

Speed and fluency are the last refinement of motor control that occurs. Once postural control, accuracy and precision of movement are in place, speed and fluency will follow. **Speed** refers to how fast an object is moving over time (Boundless Chemistry, 2014). Another way of describing **motor speed** is the rate and quality by which information is processed (Eckert, Keren, Roberts, Calhoun, & Harris, 2010).

Another example of a daily living activity: eating. Imagine your child as he/she was learning to use a fork or a spoon. When you first introduced the utensil on their plate, they probably just held it in their hand. They may have imitated you to try to use it. However, they likely held that spoon for several weeks before trying to even get it in their own mouth. The first trials were probably over shot as they found their cheek instead of their mouth.

Remember, the child has been putting their hand to their mouth since birth. Even though the spoon is only a few inches longer, your child's brain needs time to shift the accuracy of those few inches to reach his/her mouth. With the spoon finally making it to the mouth, it was probably sideways or upside down, and had no food on it. It took practice to precisely place the spoon in the mouth properly.

By the time your child was going to school, neuro-typical children usually can manage the speed and fluency of a fork and spoon efficiently to eat lunch. A knife may take more time though.

All humans, regardless of development, use this same sensory-motor system to create smooth movement with every task we perform, even the automatic tasks like breathing or the beating of our heart. From the moment we are conceived, and the fetus is forming, it begins the task of integrating the sensory stimuli around it with a motor response.

Handwriting Connection

So, how does motor function relate back to handwriting? When using a three – lined paper, an early elementary student should write his/her capital letters by touching the top line and touching the bottom line. As my friend, Beverly Moskowitz would say,

> "It must touch the top line, it must touch the bottom line. It can't go higher, it can't go low. And, it can't float in the middle." (Moskowitz, 2015, p. 46)

Another program, Handwriting Without Tears (HWT), also uses song to help students concur how to begin writing letters. Their song states:

> Where do you start the letters? At the top!
> Where do you start the letters? At the top!
> If you want to start a letter,
> Then you better, better, better
> Remember to start it at the top"
> (Olsen & Knapton, 2008, p. 20)

The use of song adds a visual, auditory, tactile, proprioceptive, vestibular, and kinesthetic component to prepare for handwriting. Each song has its own motions.

Encoding: The Motor Pathway

Students having trouble connecting his/her letters appropriately on the page are having difficulty with eye and hand coordination.

Not all children have difficulty with handwriting. However, today's curriculum is moving at such a fast pace, some children are not getting enough time to process what is being presented to them.

If a child is having difficulty with accuracy, you may find:

- gaps in the letters where gaps do not belong
- Points where curves belong
- Curves where points belong

If a child is having difficulty with precision, you may find:

- Improper use of the lines on the paper provided
  - Baseline and top line are used inappropriately (there is no top line in HWT)
  - Middle line is used when incorrectly
- Letters are formed improperly

If a child is having difficulty with speed and fluency, you may find:

- He is concentrating too intently on the placement of the letter on the page.
- He is having difficulty recalling how a letter is formed

Several handwriting programs can provide strategies to help students if they struggle in this area. Please check out Appendix C for a listing of them.

The goal of handwriting remediation in occupational therapy is to help students become accurate and precise in their pencil control to form proper letters followed by speed and fluency. Motor control is built on the accuracy and precision of the letter formation. Accuracy and precision are the foundational motor components of visual memory. Without accurate and precise motor control, speed and fluency will be limited.

When normal development and integration of the sensory-motor system does not occur, sensory processing disorders (or sensory integration disorders) are exhibited. These reactions can be applied to ALL sensory-motor systems: the visual, hearing, taste, smell, touch, proprioceptive, vestibular, kinesthetic, stereognosis, and graphesthesia systems. More information about books on sensory processing disorders is available in Appendix B.

Chapter Eight

Decoding: Vision

SINCE VISION IS 50% of what our brain processes, let's take some time and understand how the body is working with the brain to create a picture for our mind (Amen & Amen, 2017).

When I was in kindergarten, I had trouble in school seeing the books to read the words and I was left handed. Back in the 1970s when I was in elementary school, the differences that we have grown accustomed to, like glasses and writing with the left hand, were as not accepted as they are today. Being mocked without guidance for social interaction led me to withdraw into myself. I found solace from being alone because I was afraid to speak up. I was clumsy. I had difficulty playing ball. When it came to writing, I would get stuck on how to spell some words. I had difficulty expressing my thoughts, and so was also afraid to answer questions. Once I was on my own, I began the search of "What's wrong with me?" The profession of occupational therapy was only the beginning of me understanding myself.

Visual Acuity

My lack of visual acuity led me to wearing glasses. **Visual acuity** is the ability to perceive text of a certain size at a certain distance. A lack of visual acuity can be corrected to 20/20 vision with glasses. The image that the eye is detecting on the retina is not centered in the right location. If a person can see things well when they are close, he or she is considered near-sighted; if he or she sees things better far away, far-sighted. A local ophthalmologist with a specialty in pediatric visual perception can identify more specific details of each condition. By the time my parents had realized that visual acuity was a problem, other students had realized that I had a problem, too. To this day, I have difficulty focusing on the written word, unless it is in large print with lots of white space between the lines of print. Being on this earth over five decades, even my bifocals get moved down my nose to adjust the refraction of the image in front of me. My son picks on me that I wear my glasses half way down my nose. Some days I wish that going to the eye doctor would result in glasses that really worked. Even now, I'm still learning to adjust to my ocular needs. Lately, I am realizing that computer glasses are a must.

My oldest child has worn bifocals since elementary school. Her eyes do not move toward her nose to focus on close objects at

Figure 24 Therapist with child

the same rate and her distance vision is skewed due to near-sightedness. I am also very near-sighted. When your eye doctor examines your eyes and prescribes a prescription for your glasses or contacts, visual acuity is their primary target. It takes a specially trained clinician to look at the how the brain impacts our interpretation of the visual images we see. Eye doctors receive special training to go beyond visual acuity. Occupational therapists (OTs) are trained to analyze how we interpret what we see and how the interpretation impacts our daily life. OTs do not assess visual acuity, but some eye doctors can assess the interpretations of what we see. The interpretations are classified in a category called **visual perception**.

Ocular Motor Function

When we assess the motor output of the eyes, we call it **ocular motor function**. Our eyes work best together when the muscles attached to each eye work simultaneously.

We all know that we have two eyes but see only one image. How does that work? As we delve into vision a bit further, we must first understand a bit about the eyes themselves before we can look at what the brain does with the images that we see.

Each eye has six muscles that permit it to move left, right, up, down, and diagonally. They are supposed to work together in what is also called **eye teaming**.

If the muscles in each eye are not working equally and together, the eyes will not appear in the same location in the eye socket. When the eyes are not in alignment with one another, the condition is called **strabismus** (Sheiman, 2002). One eye can turn in, out, or up. At times, this condition can be severe. Eventually, the one eye does not move. A child with an eye that does not move, a so-called "lazy eye," will have poor depth perception or awareness. Depth perception is how we can tell an image is farther away or close. Imagine you're sitting on the porch? Your eyes automatically interpret whether a tree is closer or farther away.

When a "lazy eye" condition is subtle, it can result in double vision. Double vision is a like seeing words on a page with a shadow. This image demonstrates several ways a person with double vision may perceive a line of text (Randhawa, 2013).

Figure 25 Double Vision (Randhawa, 2013)

It is difficult for children to be aware that this condition exists, because they are unaware of vision in any other manner. It needs to be described to them by a trained optometrist.

Convergence and Divergence

Another area that creates problems if the muscles are not working well together, are the concepts of convergence and divergence. Let's try a demonstration exercise.

CONVERGENCE EYE MUSCLE TEST

1. Hold a pencil in your fisted hand.

2. Hold your arm extended directly in front of your eyes.

3. Move the pencil toward you.

4. When you see two pencils, stop.

5. Measure the distance of the pencil from your nose. It should be around 5-6 inches. It may be farther but should not be closer.

6. If the distance is closer, consult with a visual perceptional professional is advised.

7. Now, move the pencil to a full extended arm. Now, bring the pencil slowly towards your eyes until you see two pencils.

Feel what your eyes are doing. They are both coming toward your nose.

This concept is **convergence.** We need our eyes to converge well to read, write, and use a computer. The typical distance for a person to read a book is approximately 16-inches with the head slightly tilted forward. Computer distances and angles are slightly farther from the eyes and in more of a vertical plane.

Shift your eyes quickly look at something 10-feet or more away from you. Feel how your eyes have moved. This concept is **divergence.** Your eyes are moved more to the center of your eye socket when this happens.

There are times in which your eyes are unable to shift back and forth between convergence and divergence. Try looking and concentrating on a dot on a piece of paper, then look up at a picture on a wall around 15-feet from where you are seated. Do this by focusing on each item for 10 seconds. Repeat it until you are tired. Now consider the child that has a delay in the ability to see the dot or picture clearly within the first second.

Imagine how frustrating it must be to look up to the board and not see what you saw the last time you looked up. There are many children who must start at the beginning of what is on the board, scan through the material to find where they were, then do the next step.

You were asked to change your eye position within 10 seconds. Consider what it would be like to have to take that long to even see the board clearly? What if it takes an additional 15 seconds to scan the material on the board to find where he/she was and relate that material to what is on the paper in front of them. This ability to look back and forth from the paper and board quickly (or even left to right and top to bottom on the paper) is **visual scanning**. Children are required so many times in elementary classrooms to copy from the board and put what the teacher says in the right place on their paper.

If their eyes are having difficulty managing convergence and divergence, this task will cause frustration. Some signs that the child is struggling with scanning his/her environment could be, but are not limited to squinting, rubbing his/her eyes, staring for a long time, and not finding his/her place on the board or paper. Another way to tell is if the child looks directly over his/her paper or looks too close to the paper. Other items to keep in mind: if the child moves his/her whole head and body as one big unit and cannot turn head to side or move eyes without moving his/her head. Have an eye doctor or occupational therapist evaluate the child to determine more closely if there is truly a convergence and divergence problem.

Table 3 Convergence and Divergence

Signs of Convergence Insufficiency	Signs of Divergence Insufficiency
• Difficulty finding his/her place on a worksheet • Squinting • Rubbing eyes often • Looks at a worksheet and moves whole body to read entire sheet • Complains of eye pain	• Squinting when looking at the board • Trouble finding place when far copying • "I can't find it" • "I'm lost" • Shows signs of anxiety

There is one last concept regarding eye control, nystagmus. **Nystagmus** is the overflow of movements that your eye does when you spin.

Your vestibular system and eyes are connected. It is the job of the vestibular system to tell your brain where your head is. Children that have difficulties with their vestibular system will be the same students that are moving all day long. Children that have a vestibular system that tells them to run and hide will be afraid of many locations that have open areas like stairwells and hilly playgrounds. The occupational therapist is trained to understand the signs and symptoms of how to adjust the environment to keep all children safe and improve engaging them in classroom activities.

It is possible to have a child with both convergence and divergence issues plus nystagmus. You will need to have a sensory program designed to help you and the child's neural system grow to enjoy the classroom and be able to participate in seat work.

The explanations above are brief and simple explanations of how your eyes work. This system is neurologically complex, and it encompasses many portions of the brain.

Contrast Sensitivity

The last section of this chapter is not associated with eye teaming. However, it is impacted by how much light hits the fovea of the retina. Too much or too little impacts one's ability to see clearly. Have you ever been sun blind for a few minutes or tried to see in a dark room? The sensitivity that our retina has on filtering the light is contrast sensitivity. **Contrast sensitivity** is the ability to see objects in reduced lighting situations. This ability affects many senior citizens with poor lighting in their homes. However, many people are sensitive to overly bright lighting too. Many children cannot tolerate the brightness of a classroom and their eyes fatigue, which disengages their brains from the learning process. Sometimes worksheets printed on white paper create too much reflection, thus making it difficult to see the worksheet. Changing the color of the paper reduces eye fatigue and improve the ability to engage in learning.

In summary, each eye has ocular motor muscles that control how they move. These muscles must work together for accuracy in visual images to be received on the retina. The visual neural system sends these images to the occipital lobes. Problems with these coordinated muscle movements can result in strabismus, nystagmus, convergence and/or divergence insufficiency, or contrast sensitivities.

Learning Connection

If someone's eyes are not working well together the above reactions may occur, but how can a person's eyes impact their daily life or handwriting? First, they may appear to stare at other people or objects, regardless of where they are focused. Sometimes the delay in eye muscle movements may interfere with social norms in this way. This fixation on an object may be a way for the brain to be strengthening the eye muscles. However, when fixation becomes so much of a habit, it can prevent other necessary interactions such as proper eye contact when talking with someone.

In addition to visual scanning, the field of vision may impact a person's ability to scan his/her environment. Typically, we can see approximately 180°, with 130° being the most prominent area. Some children have difficulty seeing their full range without moving their head.

These two diagrams demonstrate what our eyes see when we are looking directly ahead of ourselves. Yes, we can see out the side of our eyes. However, the 60° center arc is the major part of our visual field.

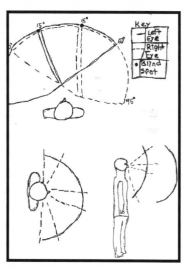

Figure 26 Visual Fields

Chapter Nine

Decoding Memories

AFTER THE INITIAL sensation makes its way from the part of the body that sensed the light touch on the arm, the vision of a tree in the distance, or a sound of a bull frog in the lake, the sensory response travels up the nervous system through the brainstem, limbic system, cortex, prefrontal cortex, and back down to the basal ganglia. After the sensation has been synchronized, the basal ganglia send messages back through the brainstem and back to the location on the body. The motor response could incorporate more areas of the body to respond than just the area of contact; the entire body responds to a single sensation.

Remember that the hippocampus holds the memory of that sensation for about 24 hours. The process of reaction to the sensation becoming a memory is divided into three basic stages. The first stage is the fraction of a second of the actual sensation occurrence.

Your hippocampus also holds that moment for a fraction of a second.

To be able to use that sensation for an activity, the hippocampus temporarily stores the working memory. Imagine trying to memorize the phone number or name of someone you just met. It takes practice for this working memory stage to truly hold the material efficiently. Our brains typically store seven digits of related data as one memory byte. That's why a seven-digit phone number was used years ago.

While you sleep, the delta stage or REM sleep converts short-term memories held in the hippocampus into long term memories. Every moment of your day will be recorded. Every moment of your hair follicles being moved by the wind will be recorded. Every breathe you made throughout the day, every beat of your heart. While you can't recall every heartbeat, your brain can.

Visualize yourself in a wooded area, the campfire is going, the tent is pitched, and you are making hot dogs over the open flames. Think about what you are seeing, hearing, smelling, tasting, and touching. Crunch, snap, grunt. That sounded like a human voice? It's getting closer?

Just then, you see one of the camp owners emerge from around the corner. "Oh, hi guys. I was just checking out something back there. No need for alarm."

As the story began were you visualizing yourself in a camp chair? Was it mid-August or early October? Were you dressed in long sleeves or short sleeves? Were you wrapped in a blanket or was it hot and muggy? Was it daytime or after dark?

Did your sensations change as the noise was mentioned? Did you feel your head move toward that sound? How about your neck, did you feel it tense?

Did you feel your trunk come more erect and lean forward? What was it?

Because it was a visualization, none of the experience was real in your physical environment (unless you are reading this book while camping). It was real in your brain though. Whether you are experiencing a vision or imagining it in your mind, your mind thinks it is real. Memories of a time in which you were camping will come to your thoughts when you visualize an event. Your brain uses past experiences to create new thoughts. Long-term memory retrieved from your temporal lobes by the hippocampus is used in the moment. Your sense of vision could probably still envision the campfire, or your sense of hearing could create the sound of crickets in the background. These thoughts are not created though a sensory-motor pathway. They are memories from the past that are accessed by your hippocampus. Your hippocampus tells your basal ganglia to send a motor response that changes your interpretation of the present. No one's memory of the campfire will be the same.

Your sense of taste may have begun making your mouth water at the thought of the hotdog and beans. Your skin may have felt a warming sensation from the memory of a warm campfire. Again, this reaction is your limbic system responding to the previous memory.

Once the distant noise was introduced, did you feel your body become more alert and stiffen up? That was those hidden senses getting ready for the possible danger lurking around the corner.

Noticed that smell was not mentioned? The sense of smell is the only sensation that does not travel up the brainstem to the limbic system. The sense of smell has a neural pathway that is linked from the nose to the amygdala. Every memory has a link to the sense of smell.

You may not have felt a change in heart beat or tensing of your body. However, if you were able to visualize, you had an experiential memory that you associated with the story.

In summary, your brain takes every piece of information that we experience and puts it in long term memory. Every sight, sound, smell, taste, and touch that we experience from the moment of conception is placed in our long-term memory.

If the sensation is something that needs an immediate response, it is placed temporarily in the working memory portion of our brain, the hippocampus. It is in this portion of the brain that the sensation—whether it is visual, auditory, olfactory, gustatory, tactile, proprioceptive, vestibular, or kinesthetic—uses the working memory to process it.

These responses all occur in the subcortical areas of the brain. In other words, we do not even think about the sensation and what response should occur. The Central Nervous System (CNS) executes these reactions for us automatically. From the subcortical levels, the brain disperses the sensory responses to the highest areas of the brain, the cerebral cortex. The purpose of this section of the book is to give an overview of the sensory motor system and its relation to the physical components of handwriting.

Children with difficulty accessing their ability to visualize will have difficulty with any aspect of the writing process. They could have difficulty with letter recall, word recognition, sentence structure, or paragraph development.

Table 4 Stages of memory development from a sensation

Stage One	Sensory Memory (immediate)	• Initial response to sensory stimulation from the environment • "The routine ability to hold ongoing experiences in mind for fractions of a second." (Purves, 2012, p. 696) • Fraction of a second
Stage Two	Working (short-term) Memory	• Temporary storage and manipulation of information. • The temporary activation of data or information so that it is available for quick retrieval. • "The ability to hold and manipulate information in mind for seconds to minutes while it is used to achieve a particular goal" (Purves, et al., 2012, p. 696). • Seconds to minutes • It is the area of the brain process that gives us the ability to hold information, internalize it, and use it to guide what we do. • Typically developed individuals can hold up to seven pieces of information in this stage.
Stage Three	Conversion to Long-term Memory	• The information is consolidated or integrated into the individual's cognitive schema. • Days or years • Long-term memory conversion only occurs during sleep (takes 7-9 hours to make the conversion)

Handwriting Connection

HOLDING A PENCIL

When you hold a pencil in your hand, the pencil touches your fingers and side of your hand simultaneously. Your brain assimilates all the points of touch into one memory of holding the pencil. As you move your hand to write, the muscles in your arm move in the same motor pattern for each letter you write. Although the movements are very small, if you try to print a sentence and think about what you are feeling while copying the sentence, you will feel the muscles from your shoulder all the way to your fingers moving.

The motor control of the pencil is dependent on the feedback from the entire feedback loop from the sensory input, the brain processes, and the control your muscles have on the pencil. If the motor control is efficient, your handwriting will be legible and have an age appropriate speed. If there is an inefficient grasp on the pencil, then control, speed, and fluency will be more difficult.

MAKING A SENTENCE ON LINED PAPER

From a visual sensory perspective, the position that you hold the paper can help or hinder your legibility to write. For young children, the larger the space is to write, the easier the task will be. That is because your muscles require bigger movements at first. As your muscle movements become secured in your memories, they do not need to move as far, and the handwriting size will decrease. Handwriting without Tears (HWT) uses 2-line paper and Size Matters Handwriting Program (SMHP) paper use three-lined paper. Kindergarten paper is 1-inch high from bottom line to top line. First grade uses three-lined paper that is ¾-inch high. Second grade uses three-lined paper that is ½-inch. Third grade uses three-lined paper is 5.5/16-inch high. Once a child can control the height in third grade, the middle line is removed and the paper mimics wide rule filler paper. By the end of third grade, a child is expected to use a single line to legibly respond to questions. Some workbooks expect second graders to write on single lined paper.

The motor control between what is seen and what the hand does (eye-hand coordination) is ultimately a very complicated process. There is so much happening between the eyes, hand, brain, and muscles in less than a second.

Understanding the process is the key to moving forward. All areas of the brain are working together to make one simple letter. Once your brain has the motor functioning down, it does not need to use all its thinking power to make the letter. It then becomes a habit and the neuroplasticity of the brain begins adding other parts to the wiring of the circuitry.

The next chapter is going to dive a bit further into how the memory process builds on itself.

Chapter Ten

Decoding Visual Memory

ACCORDING TO RESEARCH, it takes 66 days for the neuroplasticity of your brain to wire the circuitry to make anything a habit (Gardner, Lally, & Wardle, 2012). That means, that if a child only had to learn how to make the letter A in that 66-day period, it would need to start bigger and work smaller. If there is a part of the brain that is not working in a typical fashion, it will take longer. At some point in the process, a person can close their eyes and see themselves making that letter A. This ability to see your experiences through your mind is called visualization and is very important when learning new material. **Visualization** is defined as "the ability to mentally manipulate a visual image" (Sheiman, 2002). Building this technique will amplify your child's potential to learn and succeed beyond school.

If your child is unable to visualize a group of letters as a specific word, it will limit reading comprehension and the interpretation of math concepts. Without a good visual memory, spelling, word recognition, and the ability to match an image on the paper that it is written on will be limited (Sheiman, 2002). Sheiman (2002) defines **visual memory** as "the ability of the child to recognize and recall visually presented information."

Since every sensory input that enters the body must be associated with an emotion for the brain to recall it later, memory is the foundation of perception. Since 50% of the brain is devoted to vision (Amen & Amen, 2017), then visual memory must be linked in some way to all memories, with auditory memory being a close second. This statement may seem counterintuitive. However, your magnificent brain does so many things without you realizing it.

Your sensory memory activates your pre-frontal cortex. Good visual memory recall requires activation of both hemispheres of the pre-frontal cortex (Purves, et al., 2012). This procedure is called **compensatory activation**. Generally, **memory** is the "encoding, storage, and retrieval of learned information." Whereas, **learning** is "the process by which new information is acquired by the nervous system and is observable through changes in behavior" (Purves, et al., 2012, p. 695). There are two categories of memory, declarative and procedural.

Declarative Memory

Memories that can be grouped by events, images, or history are included in declarative memory. **Declarative memory** is "the storage and retrieval of material that is available to consciousness and can in principle be expressed by language (i.e. declared)" (Purves, et al., 2012, p. 695). Words and their meanings are included in declarative memory. We declare that a word means something specific. Sounds are "declared" by the experiences. For example, what does it mean when the "bell rings?" It could be that class is ready to begin or dinner is ready. The different frequencies and contexts of the sound determine the specific meaning.

Comedians understand this concept well. They know how to time their words to sway the meaning of the audience. They use events and visualization to establish the image or history.

Procedural Memory

Not all memories can be linked to a specific moment in time. Let's take an athlete training to be the new Babe Ruth. He cannot do one swing with the bat to become the new champion. It takes years of practice to train your brain and muscles how to move to accurately hit the ball out of the park.

Procedural (nondeclarative) memory is defined as "Memories that involve skill and associations that are acquired and retrieved at an unconscious level" (Purves, et al., 2012, p. 695). Go back in your mind to the point in time in which your toddler was learning to walk. He/she did not learn that task in one day. It took several months of trial and error until the task was mastered. After it was mastered, running was not that far behind.

Every time your child stood up, his/her brain registered it as a memory. Each attempt built on that memory. Once the task was made into a habit, the automatic reaction to get up and walk became a procedural memory. It went from a conscious process to an automatic event. Motions that become second nature to your brain are procedural memories. Just like the name suggests, the procedure for walking happens using the same neural pathways every time.

Some examples of procedural memories include answering your cell phone, singing a song you learned as a child, driving to and from the grocery store from home, or even playing tic-tac-toe. Once you have learned how to do the task, there may be slight changes to circumstances of that day, but the overall procedures of the task are the same. Each game of tic-tac-toe may be different, but the rules don't change.

However, if you don't use it, you lose it. That is why a ballerina or baseball player must keep practicing daily. That is why daily exercise is so important.

Effective recall of declarative and procedural memories may be spontaneous or may require an intentional reason to recall them. Dr. Larson has a three-step process that he has proven works for intentionally recalling material that is required for academic performance. They are elaborative encoding, active recall, and spaced repetition.

Elaborative Encoding

According to Dr. David Larson (2017), listening to the same playlist while doing a certain activity will create a code and activate your brain for the task you are about to complete. While Dr. Larson was in medical school, he began a method of memorizing the material that he was required to learn to graduate. He realized that by connecting new information to old information that it was much easier to recall the information. He calls this **elaborative encoding**. Encoding is the process in learning in which you respond with a verbal or written response. By repeating the process frequently, he observed that he recalled more information. He visualized old information to incorporate the new information and used songs and changed the lyrics to maximize his learning and memory power.

How many times have you crammed for a test and can't recall the information later in the month? Dr. Larson did not want to forget any of this learned information; he wanted to be sure that the neural pathways stayed active. Research has shown that your neural pathways will change every 30 days throughout your lifetime. When I was in college in the 1980s, they thought that your brain stopped creating pathways once your brain stopped growing. Neuroscientists now know that to be false. Your brain will change until the day you die by growing new neural pathways. As you change your habits, your neural pathways will reroute themselves.

NASA did a study with potential astronauts. They provided them with glasses that made them see upside down. The potential astronauts were required to wear them for 30 days. The purpose of the study was to help astronauts assimilate to space environments. Around day 25, something amazing happened. The people in the study began reporting that everything around them was like they would normally see. The brain created new neural pathways and switched the world to right side up even with the glasses intact (Canfield, 2017). This experiment has been repeated and what researchers now know is that your brain is constantly creating new neural pathways, just as the GPS system in your car is constantly in the process of rerouting you on the most efficient course to your destination. Neuroscientists have also discovered you will lose a neural pathway within 30 days if you don't use it.

Active Recall

Going back to Dr. Larson, the second step of his memorization tool is active recall. **Active recall** is the ability to use your notes without looking at them (Larson, 2017). He suggests two ways to accomplish active recall. First, teach it to someone else. When writing this book, I exercised this skill, I am actively recalling my mental notes. Yes, at times I am looking up material. However, that is part of the process. Knowing where to find details if you have forgotten them is just as important.

Second, Dr. Larson suggests creating flashcards. He copied his textbooks and created the cards from the pages. He would review them until he had every word memorized.

Spaced Repetition

Step three of Dr. Larson's method is spaced repetition. **Spaced repetition** uses the idea of studying one hour per day on a specific section of learned material. Once he was able to recall it, he continued to review the material. Over time, he spread out the material to review and integrated it with material from other parts of his semester. What I mean is, he would review the material weekly until he recalled every bit of information. After that he moved those cards to the monthly review pile. If he forgot any part of the information, he would put the material back into the daily, then weekly, then monthly piles accordingly. Remember, if you don't use a neural pathway of information, you will lose it. So, by the time he was ready to take a final in that class, he has an entire file of notes from that class and could recall the entire textbook because he was reviewing all the material constantly.

How was he building new information into his daily routine and rotating the monthly material? He spent 1-2 hours per day on active recall and 2 hours maximum on spaced repetition (Larson, 2017).

You may be thinking, "My child doesn't seem to recall anything. How can we change that?" Everyone can recall; however, it may take your child longer than another child, but he or she can do it! Finding methods that include action with vision and hearing will enhance the recall and often make it easier.

How can we teach children active recall and spaced repletion?

As I mentioned, all children have a sensory-motor response. Some children develop the ability to integrate the sensory-motor response with active, working memory at a slower pace than others. Today's education system moves at a pace too fast for many children, while it is much too slow for accelerated learners. Schools have attempted to find a happy medium, but each child is an individual and has his/her own pace. For those that have difficulty with the pace set by the schools, life can be a real nightmare for the child, parents, and teachers. Don't get me wrong, we all need to participate in active recall and spaced repetition. For most of the parents reading this book, you are in the percentage of parents whose child is having difficulty. You are here because you are looking for help. Remember, you are not alone. Many other teachers, occupational therapists, and parents are also looking for help.

As mentioned earlier, the hippocampus stores the working memory, but all areas of the brain work together to make meaning out of the memory. The goal in education is to have the child regurgitate "stuff" that he/she has been learning through a test. However, the child must be motivated to actively recall the information.

Without active recall and motivation, the child will be unable to learn the material. Remember, the information enters the neural pathways through the brainstem and moves first to the limbic system. The limbic system will take the information and pair it with old memories to develop new memories. Learning the material will only take place when the information is able to be recalled.

If you are teaching a child the alphabet, he/she might associate the learning of the alphabet with the hug that goes along with sitting next to him/her on the sofa. He/she will also find comfort in sharing the new information with their favorite stuffed toy by applying what they have learned and teaching it to the toy in spaced repetition.

Figure 27 Mom with child

Once the child is in the classroom, they find themselves on a chair with a table or desk. Their stuffed toy is at home with mom. There is no blanket to keep them warm. Transitioning from the home environment to a school situation can be less than appealing for some students. Teachers have a challenge in trying to encourage students to engage in learning.

Motivation in the classroom comes in the form of "follow the rules and do your homework and you will have fun or earn a reward." That is why a sensory-based approach to kindergarten and the early years of elementary school is so crucial. Interventions like colorful wall hangings, small group instruction, creative play-based centers, lots of interactive movement and songs, and other strategies are used by teachers to help students engage in learning.

Muscle memory

This term **muscle memory** is a synonym to motor learning. However, in recent years, it has been used in the health and wellness field to describe the building of muscle mass. Combining the two ideas can help us understand hand strengthening and endurance for handwriting. The central nervous system is building the neural pathway. Once it is built, the student can write a letter or word spontaneously. Building the muscle mass or hand strength and endurance in the fingers will help the child overcome cramps and pain responses. In short, think of muscle memory as the neuromuscular connection between your brain and any motor task involving the skeletal system, handwriting included. Motor Learning Theory is the scientific model used as the foundation of muscle memory (Gundersen, 2016).

Movement Connection

This is one reason why the computer has been such a huge success. It creates motivation on the screen through movement, visual, and auditory stimuli mixed together to create this new world of education.

When memory neural pathways are intact and developing normally, children take what is taught in the classroom, move it to the hippocampus, and convert it to long term memory while sleeping. However, some children just cannot convert memories efficiently. Their neural pathways need more repetitions to convert the message to a long-term memory. For these children, there is most likely confusion in the visual and auditory input.

PART THREE

Mechanical Dysgraphia

Chapter Eleven

Encoding VSD

BEFORE WE INVESTIGATE how our interpretation of what we see impacts reading, writing, and math. Visual-Spatial Dysgraphia (VSD) deficits include decrease symbol recognition, difficulty drawing or painting, and unusual letter formation. Their strengths are fine motor skills, musical rhythm, and they benefit from visual cueing.

The sensory stimulus is what is being sent to the brain. The messages returning from the brain create a motor response—an action performed by our muscles.

Visual perception is simply the interpretation of sensory stimuli that are being processed by the brain at any given moment in time. The most basic term associated with visual perception is visual discrimination. **Visual discrimination** is simply telling the differences and similarities between two similar objects or symbols. All the terms discussed with visual perception truly fall into this category. Have you ever done one of those diagrams in a newspaper or *Highlights* magazine that asks you to tell what is different between the picture on the left and the picture on the right? You are using your visual discrimination ability to decipher the answer. A great activity to enhance visual discrimination are hidden picture worksheets.

The brain's ability to understand the physical, virtual, mental, cultural, and social environment begins with vision. According to the American Occupational Therapy Association (AOTA), the physical environment is all buildings, furniture, plants, animals, geographic terrain, and apparatus that we use in our environment as a tool, a car for example. The virtual environment is any form of communication. It can be through TV, radio, cell phone, computer and computer programs, or photographs. The mental environment is anything that originates in the brain. It can be a thought, mental image, or even a sensory-motor reaction. The cultural environment is the customs, beliefs, patterns of behavior, expectations of society. Finally, social environments are the presence of relationships with other people (AOTA, 2014). These environments can positively and negatively impact how your brain interprets what is seen by the retina. How your brain interprets the five environments is called **visual-spatial relationships**.

Visual-spatial relationships are the ability to perceive the relationship of an object's position in an environment (Eye Can Learn, n.d.). Neural connections from the eye to the occipital lobes and the visual cortex complete this process. In the visual cortex, messages are also sent to many other parts of the brain. Some areas tell the brain how much light is coming through the eyes to the retina. Other areas perceive the form and shape of objects. A third area processes the motion of objects that are seen. After being sent to other areas of the brain, they have a motor response, and ultimately end up landing in the memory sections of the brain. This concept of visual spatial relations can be divided into several more specific terms.

The first term, **Visual-spatial awareness** includes an organized mental picture of the physical environment (Eckersley, 2012). Another example is knowing where a bookshelf is in your bedroom even though you are in your kitchen talking about its location to a friend. You have a mental image of your room and its contents. Describing the location of a book to a friend, not only uses visual-spatial relations, but also visual memory.

Have you ever noticed yourself closing your eyes to imagine where something is so that you can describe its location to someone else? They then go and attempt to get the object, and it is right where you said it would be. That is also a way of describing visual-spatial awareness. Are you beginning to see the picture? Visual-spatial relationships or awareness are very closely linked to your visual memories.

To help you remember the areas of visual spatial relationships, I have grouped them into related areas. When you are completing a worksheet, the material on the page is usually two-dimensional. With some creativity and artwork, you can change drawings to be three dimensional. I am not talking about photography or looking at your physical environment. Instead, I am talking about how information on a classroom worksheet or on the board appears as a child is trying to visually interpret what he/she is seeing.

Worksheets with typeset information and no graphic images are most often, two-dimensional. To describe two-dimensional spatial relationships, I have coined the acronym **P-FOLD**:

Position in Space
Form Constancy
Orientation
Laterality
Directionality

Position in Space

Position in space is a general term for referencing the location of an object on the page or the physical environment. Is the object to the left? To the right? Above? Below? Over? Under? Around? Position in space encompasses all types of directions. Many teachers are aware of the term Boehm Concepts. **Boehm concepts** are any words that describes a relationship to something else. Examples of Boehm concepts include opposites like over and under, front and back, inside and outside, and up and down.

Figure 28 Analog Clock

That is also what position in space describes. Have you ever tried to teach a child how to read an analog clock? With today's trend of the digital style clock being the norm, the analog is not as prevalent, even in the home. Schools still have analog clocks, but many are converting to digital clocks. However, many elementary teachers request analog clocks remain for teaching purposes.

How would you describe the time 10:12? The long hand is between the 2 and the 3 and the shorter, fatter hand is near the 10, right? The terms 'between' and 'near' describe the positions the clock hands are in space.

Geography is another example of position in space. Teaching your child how to read the legend and comprehend the concepts of North, South, East, West, and their combinations are position in space terms.

When creating a matching worksheet, you may need to say the animals are along the left side of the page and the word that matches it is on the right side. We frequently use left and right to describe something's position in space.

Form Constancy

Visual form constancy is the ability to mentally move objects around (Eye Can Learn, n.d.). The object can change shape, size, or orientation (also known as reversals), but is still the same object or form. One company has made the idea of reversal a trademark of this brand identity. I am talking about Toys R Us and Babies R Us. You understand the R in their logo is reversed (Marianek, 2017).

Figure 29 Toy R Us/Babies R Us logos

Visual Form constancy is looking at the stimulus to determine if it is larger, smaller, facing left, facing right, upside down, in bold print or a different font, etc.? Let's look at this picture for a moment.

Figure 30 Form Constancy horse

The image is the same horse, only it is in different locations, sizes, and positions. The same could be true about portraits. In these two images, it's the same child, but he is looking the other direction.

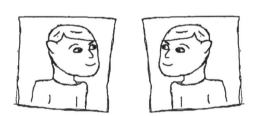

Figure 31 Boy looking both directions

The same effect occurs with symbols. **Symbols** include anything that maintains meaning in written form. Letters, numbers, and shapes are symbols. Nomenclature that goes with much of the scientific data to label it are symbols, like e=mc2. Each letter in the equation means something beyond the letter; they are symbols.

TYPESET

The FORM is constant; the size, shape, and location vary. Hence, form constancy.

Figure 32 Hashtags

All four of these symbols are the number sign. Four different fonts were used. Did you notice the subtle differences in the shape? The form is the same, the shape is different.

Figure 33 Four a in different fonts

The same is true about these four symbols. If you notice, the symbol for this letter is made two different ways. Changing this font can confuse children just learning how to read.

I have a child on my caseload that does not understand that these two different ways of creating the symbol for the sound we say "a" can be written in both manners. Again, the differences in the typeset, handwritten and computer-generated fonts, is very important when designing worksheets for students having visual spatial relationship difficulties.

Figure 34 Reversals and mirror images

These letters seen in reverse have a constant form. In the first two examples, the same form with a different orientation is understood as two different letters. This can cause difficulties even for emergent learners who do not have any visual difficulties, because it goes against what they are taught in all other subjects- a triangle is always a triangle, no matter which way you turn it; 3 corners and 3 sides makes a triangle, no matter whether it's big or small, has the point facing up, down, left, or right.

When talking with other parents and a teacher who is an Orton-Gillingham reading specialist, they reported difficulty with the lowercase letter g as shown written 'g' versus a g written 'g' and distinguishing between an 'l' and 'i' in some typewritten documents. The form constancy in these letters is not equal.

Figure 35 Cat in several fonts

This example shows "cat" in various fonts. The differences may not impact everyone. However, the change in font can be enough to make a familiar reading passage something foreign. Keep letter font sizes and shapes in mind when teaching reading and handwriting to reduce form constancy discrepancies.

NOTE: This font is the **Century Gothic** font. Please note that the 'a' and the 'g' resemble Zaner-Bloser, the style of printing most commonly taught in schools. It is also publications approved.

Figure 36 Sample Century Gothic font

COINS

Do you understand how changing the shapes, sizes, locations, and orientation of things that are observed could confuse some children? Let's look at money for a moment. Dollar bills have the same form constancy. However, coins have different sizes. Each coin is round, making the form constant. However, the edges of each are slightly different. The differences can be an overwhelming for some children to grasp. Since the change on the appearance of the quarter and nickel, I even need to stop and clarify which coin is in my hand.

Now, try to change it up for practical reasons. Give the child play money. These coins are not anything like real money. Manufacturers have tried to make the plastic molds the same, but they just are not alike. Another way that coins and money education is made difficult for some students is the two-dimensional representation of coins on a page. Pencil drawings are sometimes hard to interpret if a child has visual spatial awareness issues.

Orientation

Simply put, another name for **orientation** with respect to handwriting is reversals and mirror images. Are the letters written in the reverse direction? As noted earlier, this is especially tricky with letter pairs such as b-d, p-q, and u-n.

Laterality

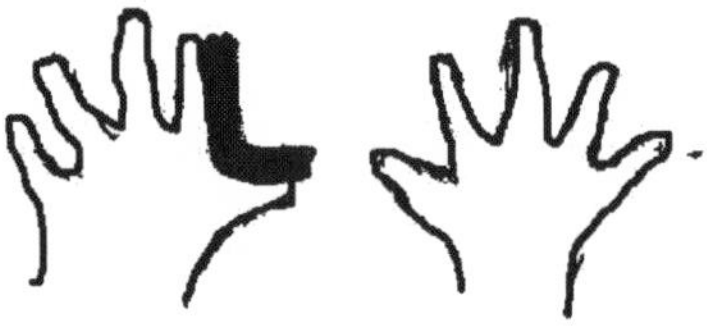

Figure 37 Left - right discrimination on hands

How many people hold both hands in front of themselves with their thumb out to figure out which side is left and right? For those that this concept doesn't comes naturally, here is an explanation.

Place both hands in front of you with the palms down or away from you, thumb out. Your left hand will make and L in the correct direction and your right hand will be a reversal. Many children need to have this visual to figure out the difference between which hand is the left verses right. **Laterality** is another way of describing left and right. It is possible to interchange **left-right discrimination** for this term.

If a child is told to put an X to the left side of a table on a worksheet, they may need more understanding of the Boehm concepts and not be aware of their left and right. Conquering this understanding will make handwriting tasks much easier. When writing in English, we write left to right. In other languages, that may not be the case. Chinese may be written vertically, and Hebrew is written right to left for example.

Incorporating exercises to strengthen laterality or left-right discrimination can be done easily in situations around the classroom. Be sure that the child is positioned so that the student can easily make the connection. Don't tell a student that something is to the left when they must look at it from the front and facing it. The easiest way to explain left and right is to orient oneself in the same direction as the student. Turn your back to your student or stand alongside him/her to teach left and right. Understanding this concept while facing each other is too difficult for most children, and even many adults. How often do people incorporate hand gestures while giving directions to a landmark? Some may even create a handwritten map. It is much easier to explain if the people involved are facing the same direction.

For example, understanding left and right while learning a new dance is imperative. When teaching it, most times the choreographer must teach a dance with his/her face away from the dancer so that the dance moves are identical to those of the instructor.

Directionality

Directionality is generalized to any direction that an object is from another object. The object can be up or down, in front of or behind, over or under, etc. This term can be interchanged with Position in Space. The following is a three-dimensional example. Consider thinking about the refrigerator as a picture looking at it from the open door as a drawing on a worksheet.

When putting a container of milk in the fridge the other day, I needed to place it on its side. My son was unable to locate the milk because he could not see the milk hiding right in front of his nose. All he saw was the lid. He could not make the connection that the milk container was on its side. The directionality of the milk container was not a typical placement. He missed the object based on directionality.

MULTI-STEP MULTIPLICATION PROBLEMS

Accurately lining up numbers is a task that creates so much anxiety for some children; they just shut down. Adding zero for place value can help. However, if the problem adds additional digits, children do not understand where to put the additional place values. For some children, using graph paper or turning lined paper sideways so that they can use a different color line as place value guides can be helpful.

FRACTIONS

Adding fractions into mathematic problems is visual spatial. In addition to the math concepts of creating the ratio, the appearance of one number over another can create confusion for children. Does the numerator belong on the top or the bottom?

Using position in space, form constancy, orientation, laterality, and directionality it is possible to identify the position of objects with relationship to other objects. **P-FOLD** is an acronym to help you recall these terms.

We've discussed ocular motor function and visual spatial relationships and how they impact education and daily life, but there are a few other aspects of visual perception that we have not discussed. These areas are visual closure, visual figure ground, and depth perception. These two concepts deal more with an object being on top of another object. They have a three-dimensional nature.

Visual Closure

Visual closure is the ability to visualize a complete whole when given incomplete information or a partial picture (Eye Can Learn b., n. d.). Picture worksheets that have ½ the picture and the child must draw the remaining half are examples of visual closure. Visual closure also applies with dot to dot style drawings. The drawing must be finished to reveal what the picture is.

COMPLETE THE PHOTO

About a month after I was married, my mother had what is best described as a stroke in her eyeball rather than in her brain. The aftermath of this occurrence was that my mom was unable to see in parts of her visual field. Her doctor told her to stand at the same place each day and consciously look at something and journal what she sees each day. She chose an 11X14 photograph of my brother, sister, and me. Each day she would look at the picture that was at the head of her bed for many years. Just after the injury, she was only able to see the left side of the photograph.

Over the next 6-12 months, she began seeing more of the picture. She knew what should be on the photograph which helped "fill in" the missing visual field.

However, using the conscious effort, she could take what was her visual memory of the picture and note what she saw each day. Now, she sees the entire picture. Her medical eye doctor has said that her visual field really has not returned. Her memory and visual closure improved her eye sight after the first 6-12 months of recovery.

Although the example is like the NASA experiment discussed in Chapter 10. It may not initially resonate with everyone. Think of how the visual field, visual memory, and visual closure could impact a child in a school environment that is new. He/she may totally be missing wall hangings or other important triggers in the classroom.

FINDING SHOES

A friend of mine told me that her child would lose his shoes in his bedroom. What happens next? "Mom, I can't find them!" She went to the room and just like magic, there they were. Think through what she did to find the shoes. Did she move anything? Did she see a corner of the shoe under a blanket? His visual closure and ability to finish what his shoes looked like under the blanket were not present in his cognitive abilities.

How does this concept impact the classroom? Does your child see the big picture or the small details? Children with visual closure struggles have a difficult time understanding what is on the page if the lettering is too small or the page is too busy; the paper looks like a black and white blur. This blur is different from the blur of visual acuity problems. When a font is too small, the page can look like lines of black amongst the white background. Color makes interpretation more difficult.

Recommendations for children with visual closure problems?

- Have them name an object when confronted with only half of its image
- Do connect the dots
- Design copying pages
- Find objects partially hidden in the bedroom
- Finish the drawing worksheets

Visual Figure Ground

Visual figure ground is the ability to pick out an object within a busy or similar background (Eye Can Learn c., n. d.). Games like "I Spy" and "Where's Waldo" are great examples of picking out objects in a busy background. A speech therapist gave me this analogy when I worked in a nursing home: Figure ground is like finding mashed potatoes on a white plate. A person needs good visual figure ground to put a 1000-piece jigsaw puzzle together. The colors are very similar, and the background is busy.

DECORATIONS IN CLASSROOM

Many teachers love to decorate their room with colors and concepts all over the place. For a child with visual figure ground difficulties, the room may be extremely overwhelming. One teacher realized that this pre-decoration of the room created anxiety-like reactions in several children, so the next year she had her students tell her where to place the visual prompting information. She noted less anxiety-like reactions the second year. This change in format may not work for all classrooms, but she made the change and included it as part of her lesson planning for the next several years and found continued anxiety reduction. She also noted that students engaged more with the visual prompts.

Suggestions to accommodate for visual figure ground issues include:

1. **Reduce figure ground by simplifying the page.** Some students cannot deal with worksheets that have several problems and colors on them. For younger grades, try redoing worksheets to have two math problems on them with a bold divider in the middle of the page. Reduce again if that is still too much.

2. **Simplify colors.** Colors can be distracting. There are some situations where simple black and white drawings are less confusing for students. Sometimes colors of the printed material are too closely similar. Increase the contrast of the colors; black and white have the greatest contrast. However, sometimes white is too reflective. Grey, or pale yellow or green can be a better choice to copy worksheets. This change may increase cost, but it may help students with these difficulties. It is worth a try.

3. **Use transparencies.** If cost is a barrier, try using a transparency in yellow, blue, or green to cover the worksheet and write answers on the transparency or on another sheet of paper. You can also attach the transparency on a craft light and use the craft light to change the contrast sensitivity and the figure ground.

4. **Change fonts and font sizes.** Increase font size for reading material or use an electronic reader such as a Kindle or Nook to provide backlighting.

Backlighting may need to be in a color other than white. Most apps allow the user to change colors.

5. **Reduce fluorescent lighting.** Use table lamps instead of florescent lighting, or deflect sunlight with window coverings. Manufacturers make florescent light covers to tone down the brightness of the lighting, which are typically made for commercial use.

Depth Perception

Depth perception is defined by Sheiman as the "ability to judge depths and distances" (2002, p. 184). Each eye sees the world at slightly different angles. The brain takes these images and creates one picture in the mind's eye. When this system is not working properly, the mind may not perceive the proper distance that an object is from another object. Depth perception is crucial in determining how far a car is from the car in front of it. The interpretation of depth tells a foot how hard to press the brake pedal to stop a potential collision with another vehicle.

Another example is baseball. The pitcher needs to assess how far the catcher's mitt is from him. The batter needs to ascertain how fast the ball is approaching so that he swings at the right moment. The outfielder needs to clarify how quickly the fly ball is coming toward him.

Depth perception is also necessary to determine how far the next step is located when walking. Is it a 6-inch step or more? Not only does mobility require depth perception, but so does understanding how far objects are from the student in school. Every time a student must look down at his paper, then up at the board to copy something, their eyes need to adjust the depth of the focus. The eyes and brain interpret how far the paper and board are from the student. The eyes move position to maximize the focus, convergence, and divergence.

Children with depth perception challenges will have difficulty determining how far, hard, or soft to throw a ball. They will also have trouble seeing the board or their paper interchangeably. The millisecond delay to focus could be their source of frustration.

Handwriting Connection

The motor learning theory plays a role here. Again, motor learning is the process of repeating the motor planning process so that the muscle movement sequences become ingrained in the child's motor memory. Remember, this motor memory can leave a positive or a negative emotion that becomes associated with the sequence. Please consider making all projects a reward and bless the positive parts no matter how small. By enhancing the motor planning with positive thoughts and gratitude, the child will become much more invested and engaged in the project.

However, motor learning will not be efficient if the child's eyes are not teaming together. Please refer to the section on ocular-motor processing to understand more of how the eyes muscles work.

Vision is the source of where the information is entering the sensory motor system if reading in a traditional matter. If someone is blind, then tactile and auditory responses are primary sources of information. People with one eye, learn to adapt. However, their depth perception can never be as accurate as a person with both eyes.

Therefore, handwriting is dependent on your eyes working well together. They need to spontaneously adjust to different shapes and forms as well as various depths. Your visual memory must help fill in the picture in your mind's eye to confirm an object if it is hiding.

Chapter Twelve

Adaptive Strategies

TREATMENT INTERVENTIONS HAVE been dispersed throughout the book. This chapter breaks down the areas of visual perception (material taken in from the environment) and visual motor integration (motor response after the brain interprets the sensation). This provides specific interventions strategies to enhance and improve weakened areas of neural development. Recall from chapter 11 the acronym **P-FOLD**: Position in space, Form constancy, Orientation, Laterality, and Directionality.

When working on a piece of paper, these terms help describe the relationships pictures and symbols have to each other on the flat surface. Position in space is the overarching term for the rest of the terms when considering a two-dimensional perspective. Form constancy is understanding that an object is the same no matter its size or direction. Examples of activities to encourage form constancy are included on the following pages.

P-FOLD Activities

Fonts can help or hinder a child's ability to understand the works on the page. Use an easy-to-read font and be consistent in using it.

Reversal awareness is the key to the orientation of letters. Finding the picture in the opposite direction is an example of finding reversals. Mirror images are a form of reversals. The reversal is vertical rather than horizontal.

When exploring form constancy, some children cannot understand the similarities between play money and real money. You may need to resort to real money in the classroom for some students.

Some schools are stating that they are taking the analog clock from the classroom. This venture will be a disservice to our children. Please consider putting the analog and digital clock side by side in each classroom. You never know when the electricity will go out. The analog clock also informs the concept of clockwise and counterclockwise. Color coded arrows surrounding the clock help.

Worksheets with visuals such as a timeline or ruler emphasize equal and unequal parts. Other resources are the manipulatives that are used in beginning math and counting. There are many ideas on the internet to emphasize this concept. Children with form constancy struggle with abstract thought. They will need physical, colorful, and potentially textured manipulatives to develop an understanding regarding these ideas.

Fractions are much the same. I had a student that was struggling with fractions. I also had an OT student at the time. My OT student created felt cutouts of the fractions to help my elementary student conquer this concept. Adding textures to the felt enhanced the younger student's understanding of the concept of fractions.

Do you still give your students worksheets that have half a picture on it and they must finish the drawing or copy a design? Fill in the blank or fill in the box exercises are similar examples. Placing the correct word in on a blank line or the proper number in an equation sentence may be difficult for students with form constancy struggles. Visualizing what the other half of the house should look like on a 'finish the picture' worksheet may be impossible for students that have difficulty determining similarities and differences to shape and size.

Jigsaw puzzles, parquetry, and tangrams are similar. Parquetry and tangrams are activities in which you take geometric shapes and create pictures from the shapes. Sometimes the student must copy a picture, and other times they can create something independent of a structured diagram. Copying a drawing by using the shapes to cover it takes different neural pathways than the creative method. Defining the shapes that are embedded in the larger shape and removing one line as the child becomes successful, will help develop their neural pathway.

Origami by design is geometric shapes built on one another. If a child has form constancy concerns, you may need to model step by step directions for them to master the origami shapes and forms.

Any two or three-dimensional manipulatives will enhance a child's comprehension of form constancy. When considering how to best engage students, think of multi-sensory experiences and tools. Play dough, shaving cream, pudding, Bendaroos™, or even dry spaghetti could be used. Be aware of allergies as you use manipulatives. Play-doh™ has gluten. Some mediums should not be used depending on setting.

Letter boards are posters that are created by the instructor to promote the identification of symbols and shapes. All that is needed is poster board and yard sale stickers. Use the following steps to complete the exercise:

- Place one letter or shape on the yard sale sticker.

- On a second sticker, place a matching letter or shape. It can be capital, lowercase, or a picture, anything that will match sticker one. Mother and baby animals can be used.

- Place them on the poster board in random locations.

- Concentrate on placing the stickers in vertical, or horizontal patterns.

- Repeat until you have the desired number of letters on the board.

Letter boards are great for building many visual perceptual neural pathways.

Any object that helps students understand that a form, shape, or symbol can be bigger, darker, lighter, or turned will support building the neural pathways for form constancy; be creative. Searching the internet for ideas will turn up an abundance of options.

Learning left and right and top to bottom concepts take a bit more cognitive skill than simply recognizing and writing letters properly. Adding the element of a verbal command for direction adds to the element of these activities. For example, while a student is completing a connect the dots puzzle and is having difficulty, instead of pointing out the next dot, give them verbal direction using the Boehm concepts.

Visual Figure Ground Activities

When developing activities, keep contrast in mind. Black on white or pastel yellow is the best contrast.

Too much detail becomes confusing. Remember, sometimes less is more when working on activities. Increasing white space will improve the student's visual awareness and ability to track and scan the material. Students with visual figure ground difficulty have a more difficult time reading chapter books with smaller fonts. They also have more difficulty writing in the small spaces provided in many worksheets. Enlarging the size of the material of the worksheets to fit on two pieces of paper will spread the information and decrease the visual figure ground.

Visual Closure and Depth Perception Activities

The lack of visual closure and depth perception awareness is a clue to the child's eyes not working together. If you have a worksheet that the child simply cannot tell you whether the cat is in front of or to the side of the bed, the child may have depth perception issues.

Eye teaming is necessary for most reading and writing activities. Difficulty with these activities could demonstrate signs of motor integration issues.

The emphasis for these activities is placed on finding objects near other objects that are partially hidden. Some examples include completing the picture worksheets, puzzles, parquetry, origami, and what's missing from the picture worksheets.

If you'd like to incorporate a gross motor activity into strengthening these areas, an outdoor scavenger hunt or finding your shoes from the pile of everyone's shoes are some ideas. An obstacle course that goes around the corner, so the student cannot see it from beginning to end will help improve visual closure and depth perception too.

Environmental Modifications

The impact of the environment has a significant impact on a child's ability to read, write, and complete other school tasks efficiently. Be aware that lighting has a huge impact on some children. Simply turning off lights and allowing the sunshine to light the room can be adequate to change the mood of the situation. Lumens can also change the impact of lighting in the room. A lumen can shift the room from blue light to orange or yellow tones in the lighting. A lumen is given off by the wattage of a light bulb. Different watts give off a different spectrum of light. That can change the whole response to a person's ability to learn. The lumen rating is located on the light bulb package materials.

Seating can make a difference in a student's ability to write efficiently. Their feet must touch the floor with a flat foot while their bottom is on the back of the chair. Change desks or seating if the desk and chair do not allow for this positioning. Many new strategies are being used in classrooms such as ball chairs, wiggle chairs, and other types of chairs. These can be used to improve posture and balance.

Locations for reading that promote lying on stomach or sitting in bean bag chairs encourage students to obtain different postures throughout the day. Different postures encourage muscle development of other areas of the body. Lying prone on one's stomach is good for students who spend much of their day with their hips bent. Having something to lie over such as a bolster will help them have comfort in this position. Independent reading time is a good opportunity to have these locations available in the room. There's nothing better than soft lights and a place to lie on your stomach or lie in a bean bag chair with a book. Also, note that students with writing difficulties have more stability in their upper body if you allow them to write from a prone posture instead of at the desk. Portable lap desks or clipboards will be necessary for an uninterrupted surface. Many floors have vinyl tile floors that will create ridges under paper, which can be difficult for students learning to write.

In summary, one activity can improve several visual perceptual and visual motor deficits. Be creative, and be aware of environmental factors that can impact learning.

Chapter Thirteen

Encoding MotorD

MOTOR DYSGRAPHIA (MotorD) is the most externally visible form of dysgraphia. These children have poor muscle tone and display clumsy behaviors.

The best way to translate the neuroscience principles of Motor Learning Theory into dysgraphia into the classroom is to think **MOVER**. Remember, motor learning theory and muscle memory are synonyms.

Motor
Ocular/Senses
Vestibular
Environment
Repeat

Designing strategic movements while preparing for writing will reinforce neural pathways and enhance the learning process. Since 50% of what our brain's process is visual, consider how to include vision in the activity alongside as many of the other four senses as possible (Amen & Amen, 2017). Engaging the hidden senses like the vestibular and proprioceptive systems will support the student's ability to create memories by engaging multiple areas of the brain. Physical, cultural, personal, social, temporal, and virtual environment integration will also improve the reinforcement of the learning process.

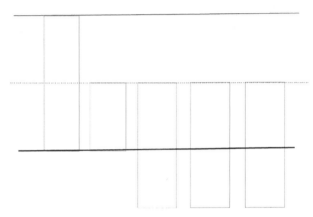

Figure 38 Happy

An idea used by occupational therapists and teachers are creating block words and filling in the appropriate letters to complete the word (the figure spells *happy*), separating the syllables and have students reconnect them. This technique is to teach reading and writing while filling in the blanks to complete the first, middle, or final sound.

Another strategy is to take the parts of the letters apart and find ways to identify a visual pattern to help students achieve success.

Vestibular Connection

Since the vestibular system and ocular motor and neck position are so interconnected, any movement activity prior to writing for children with MotorD can enhance their writing ability. Isolation of eyes from head movement can improve visual scanning.

Eye Muscle Activities

A great way to encourage eye muscles to move is visual scanning games. For example, make a chart on a poster board using the concepts explained in the Letter Board section. You can use adult and baby animals, capital and lowercase letters, number sequences. Set the chart up so that some pairs are vertical, some are horizontal, and some are diagonal. If you notice the child is always fixating up, then encourage the eyes to scan in a lower quadrant of the poster board. If he/she is fixating down, then encourage the upper quadrant of the poster. Remember, to keep the poster centrally located in front of the child

Have the child stand or sit about 10 feet from the poster. Ask them to find the adult sheep, then the baby. Use the same ideas with the letters, number, and other objects on the poster. This task should take at least five minutes to fully enforce the exercise. Just like with cardiovascular exercise, duration is important to ensure the activity sticks. If you want the child to look farther away, make the targets larger. You can also do this task at arm's length and have the child point to objects.

This activity strengths the ocular muscles and encourages them to team together. It will help improve convergence, divergence, and visual scanning.

One task that I have seen vision therapists do uses an index card. They have the child look at the card then an object several feet away. They must count to 10 before moving their eyes.

A variation on this idea is the sticker stare game. Place a sticker on an index card; then place the card in various locations in their eye path and have them stare at it for 10 seconds before moving to another location.

You can also have the child make a necklace. Place beads on a pipe cleaner or fish line. Place the beads (or ziti or anything else that can be slid down the line) at eye level and have them look down to their lap to string the beads. This activity will help work on convergence and divergence. Any variation on this theme is great.

Games that focus on fine motor skills, like Operation™ and Light Bright™, will help children with fixation problems.

Other examples of visual scanning games include:

a. Find and cross out all the a's in a word search.

b. Use arrows. Circle all the arrows facing left.

c. Find all the 2's in the room. This will encourage a farther distance.

d. Have the child go down the hall and touch targets on the left then right wall. You can try a multitude of ways to get them down the hall: walk, crawl, animal walk, etc. Encourage the opposite hand to touch the object to encourage full body movements.

e. Don't forget ceiling floor scanning and diagonal scanning too.

f. All the activities for visual spatial relationships can be used here too.

Eye-Hand Coordination Activities

As for being left-handed, I was taught how to hold my paper differently than the rest of the class. To have a teacher that understood that was a great benefit; otherwise, I may also have had more difficulty with handwriting.

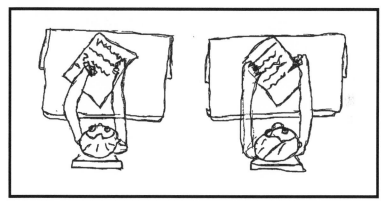

Figure 39 Paper position

A right-handed person sets up paper with the bottom left tip of the paper pointing to his/her belly. Whereas, a left-handed person should set up the paper with the right corner facing his/her torso. There was a time in which all paper was to be turned so that the left tip was facing the stomach. Left-handed persons who learned to write with the paper turned in this fashion tend to write with their wrist in flexion (bent forward). Writing with your hand in flexion will cause fatigue and hand cramps more often.

Before we look at specific ways how our vision impacts the learning process, let's go a bit deeper into the vision pathway. Do you wear glasses, contacts, or have you had laser eye surgery? If so, this information may seem familiar.

141

Classroom Connection

Children with ocular motor problems have a difficult time focusing on the board or written word. Their eyes are moving all over the place creating the inability to follow what they are reading even with their finger. By strengthening these muscles, you will not only improve reading, but also improve other eye-hand tasks like tying shoes, buttoning buttons, starting zippers, hitting a ball with a bat, etc. Ocular motor function will impact all aspects of a child's day.

Copying Material

Near point information is material copied from a paper or textbook on the desk next to the student. Far point copying is written on the board and copied to a worksheet or agenda on the desk. The student does not need to move their head in a vertical motion to obtain the next piece of data in near point copying. During far-point copying, the process of looking up at the board, then down at the paper activates the vestibular system. A child with an immature vestibular system may have significant difficulty with this task.

TYPES OF COPYING

Near Point: On surface being copied from

- Direct copy
- Copy from paper or text book above the paper
- Left or right side of copy paper

Midpoint: On computer
Far point: Five feet away or greater

If a student frequently complains of tired eyes, dizziness, getting lost on the page easily, or simply refuses to copy from the board, ask for an occupational therapy evaluation. Be sure that you include what you have noticed. In the meantime, provide material on paper for the student to add their homework to their schedule or provide the material that is on the board.

Any of the visual perceptual activities that were mentioned in the previous chapter will also benefit visual motor integration. The emphasis is to add an element to increase accuracy, precision, control, and speed.

Other things that can improve eye-hand coordination include timing the activities, increasing the length of the material to copy, making the lines of a maze closer together, gross motor eye-hand or eye-foot coordination activities with a field that narrows over time.

Books naturally do this by making the font smaller and decreasing the white space on the page. Children are also expected to read and write faster on the paper provided by the company designing the worksheets. If you have a student with dysgraphia, increase the size and decrease the amount of movement their head needs to move to improve their control, accuracy, precision, and speed. Upgrade the tasks by returning them to non-adapted forms over time.

Motor Control Activities

Controlled muscle movements are such an integral part of legible handwriting. From the muscles in your core and upper body to the muscles from your neck to your fingertips, each one has an important role. Coordinating movements of both sides of the body and controlling movements of arms crossing the middle of the body are crucial to writing across the page.

In addition, the upper body needs to be prepared for academic tasks. Activities at the side of the desk between subjects will help children transition from one topic to another. They can also be used to refocus the group after a transition back into the classroom from a special class or recess.

Games that encourage bilateral movement (arms and legs on both sides) are useful. Encouraging the student to cross the middle of their body makes these activities more beneficial.

The following pages have some examples of these exercises:

Brain Yoga is a pose that wakes up the brain by crossing midline and activating core control.

Pinch your right ear with your left index finger and thumb.

- Pinch your left ear with your right index finger and thumb.

- Squat as low as you would to sit on a toilet.

- Hold that pose 10 seconds.

- Repeat 4 times for a total of five squats.

Encourage the students to squat as low as they can go without losing their balance. Brain yoga engages both sides of the brain, activates the core and leg muscles. It is a great refocusing activity.

Brain Gym has a great program to facilitate such activities. The teacher's manual can be found here:

Dennison, P. & Dennison, G. (1989). Brain Gym:
Teacher's edition. Edu Kinesthetics. Ventura, CA
Their website: http://www.braingym.org

My favorite exercise to prepare hands for writing is the Inverted Prayer exercise. This exercise can be completed standing or seated.

- Raise arms overhead.

- Bring palms together; your hands will look like they are praying.

- Keeping the palms of your hands touching, bring your hands to your chest.

- Your elbows should bend to approximately a right angle.

- Once hands are at midline, move them left to right touching each shoulder. Keep palms together. Be sure to touch your shoulder joint with your hands.

- Repeat 4 times.

- Back at midline, turn your fingertips to the floor. Keep your palms together.

- Repeat the left-right motion. You will not move as far with your fingers pointed at ground.

- Repeat 4 times.

- Release your hands, shake out your arms, and get ready to write.

Any student that complains of hand pain that also has full active motion in their arms will benefit from this exercise.

You can modify this exercise by:

- Placing your palms on the edge of the desk.

- The bones at the base of your fingers (palm facing desk) should be the only part of your hand touching the desk.

- Push on the desk allowing your wrist to move toward the desk. You will feel a stretch in the wrist above the palm.

- Hold 10 seconds.

- Repeat 4 times.

None of these exercises should take more than 2-3 minutes to complete. These are only a few examples of total body/upper body writing preparation. As mentioned before, be creative in your ways to encourage body control before writing.

Speed and Fluency Activities

The last area is speed. Once your student has accuracy, precision, and control of his/her movements, increasing speed is the last area to tackle. This task can be graded by taking the number of letters or sentences and dividing by the number of seconds the task took to complete, then multiplying by 60 seconds. Your result should be letters per minute. Increased tolerance of time constraints with legibility indicates speed and fluency.

Think of writing in a rhythm. Each letter has a rhythm to it, as do words. Counting out the rhythm will help with the speed at which a word's spelling is learned orally. Taking that rhythm, internalizing it, and creating a mental visualization of the word, then writing it.

Speak this pattern out loud: bum, chuck, chuck, bum, chuck, chuck. Repeat it. Notice how the beat is formed in your auditory rhythm? Did you create a rhythm that had three beats per measure or did you build in a silent beat? Many programs use patterns in math and music class. However, they are not incorporated into Language Arts programs on a regular basis. Try something with your students. When you are going to teach spelling words on a Monday, ask the students to stand away from their desks. Start by clapping out a beat. Have them join you. Keep it slow. 1-2-3-4-1-2-3-4, etc. Ask the students to keep the beat. You, the teacher, add movements with each letter. Let's use the word *shopping*. You are teaching the spelling rule of adding the double consonant. Emphasizing the double consonant is key in your lesson. Using the rhythm, you established, have the students clap along. As they have the rhythm sounding uniform, add vocals to spell the word, s-h-o-p-p-i-n-g. Have students add the spelling to the rhythm. Once they have that synchronized, add movement. For consonants punch up, for vowels, punch down. For the special ending, punch forward. Repeat the rhythm stating up-up-down-up (short vocal for the double consonant)-punch forward from left to right three times (shopping). Now, use the letters to complete the process. A video for this strategy is located at www.dysgraphiaconsultant.com. It may take longer on the initial learning process, but students will pick up on it quickly.

Spelling will improve because you have added motion to embed the motivation to learn it. Besides, how much of their day is sitting? This strategy gets them moving.

Watch them during the spelling test. They will use these techniques to spell out the letters. You may need to teach the class to "do it small" for the test. For example, visualizing the motion in their mind.

Chapter Fourteen

Encoding MemD

THE PRIMARY AREA of concern with Memory Dysgraphia (MemD) is recall of new and old schoolwork. If someone has difficulty with an "easy" task, they could feel discouraged. In addition to the visual perceptual and visual motor integration frustration, the limbic system is telling the brain, "Hey, there is danger here. Be on alert." Children are not able to cognitively understand the internal responses and will need role modeling of proper social norms to overcome these behaviors. There are several people in the school system who may be able to help: guidance counselors, speech and occupational therapists, learning support or autistic support teachers, and regular education teachers.

Many children are taught strategies to enhance the five areas of reading. However, if the child is misunderstanding the form constancy of the reading material or has difficulty with directionality or laterality, the task of reading can be the most difficult task of the day and use the most energy in the brain. The child with difficulty will fatigue much sooner. A child whose brain has checked out because it needs more fuel, can lead to trouble in the classroom; motivation for learning is lost.

The brain takes what the child sees and converts it to a memory, creates a motor sequence over time to write it, and sends to the hand to write it when it is recalled into short term memory.

This information, your working memory, is stored in the limbic system in the hippocampus. To use that information in written form you need to be able to form letters, words, sentences, paragraphs, and essays.

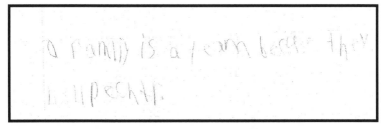

Figure 40 Sentence: A family is a team because they help each other. Student was 8 years old.

The visual memory of the word appearances is not fully integrated into the child's hippocampus. It is crucial at this time that spelling rules are taught and integrated into a child's language development. Creating videos, songs, and sayings with motions will help embed them into the visual memory. This stage incorporates teaching word patterns and phrases. Movement songs will improve recall or letters and many concepts. Separate songs for declarative and procedural concepts will help reinforce the type of memory being reinforces. Use color to assist students with organization of materials and cognitive understanding of tasks and steps.

Incorporating the thought of the other senses will deepen the visual memory of the spelling words. Take the word 'appreciate.' My daughter has the worst time spelling this word. As we were studying for her spelling test, we came up with this little saying to help her: "A priest I ate." I was not teaching her to be a cannibal, but the action of eating and activation of the taste buds and olfactory sense helped her recall the spelling. Although our sentence is not a direct correlation to the word, it worked. She still says that in her mind when spelling the word, I've been told. As of the printing of this book, she is a young adult.

Using the concepts of Spaced Repetition to ensure learning has been converted to a memory and a motivation to continue to learn. Practice Dr. Larson's method to review previously instructed concepts.

PART FOUR

Language~Cognitive Dysgraphia

Chapter Fifteen

Encoding WFD

WORD FORMATION DYSGRAPHIA (WFD) is the inability to link the patterns of letters to create words. To review, these children have great oral skills, good reading comprehension, good fine motor skills, and age appropriate oral spelling. There is a gap in taking the oral knowledge and writing it. Their alphabet memory and written spelling are dependent on phonics. They most likely have decrease hidden sensory pathways. Educators have studied frequently used words for years. Dolch and Fry have lists that encompasses the frequently used words and divided them by grade. Those that do not follow a common pattern are called sight words. Those that do follow patterns are frequently taught together. Students with dysgraphia have significant difficulty recalling sight words or word patterns.

Orthon-Gillingham programs like Barton and Wilson incorporate some of the strategies used in previous chapters. If your students still have difficulty with word formation, here are a few more strategies to try.

Spelling Rules

Nessy.com has short videos that children can watch that incorporate spelling rules. Other YouTube channels may also help teach students spelling rules. The more motion that you can include with the video, the better.

Body Sentence

A Body Sentence uses your body to create a sentence to remember spelling words or other vocabulary spellings. Many of the sight words do not follow phonic or spelling rules. The English language has so many words that have unique spellings. Some follow rules, while others disregard those rules.

One of those words is *enough*. How many of your students have a difficult time spelling words that do not follow phonics? I have a student that wants to spell the word, "E-N-U-F." Mom was frustrated with him. She had tried rote memorization, both orally and written. Rote memorization of sight words works for some students, but not all of them. Every time that she came back to the word later in the day, he spelled it phonetically, "E-N-U-F."

Being trained to make adaptations to everything around me, I was determined to figure out a method that he could use to master these words that did not follow phonetic rules.

We looked at his body to figure out what body parts began with e, the eyes and ears. He chose the 'eyes.' N came next. He chose to identify his 'nose.' Then o. The only thing we could think of was openings on your face, nostrils and open your mouth. He chose, 'open your mouth.' The letter u needed a bit more thinking. We finally chose 'under the chin.' We made the letter u by following our jaw line from ear to ear. When we arrived at g, it also took some thought. Finally, I said to him, "Give me your hand." He loved the idea of a hand shake. 'Give me your hand,' stuck. Now to end this wonderful word on a high note, we exchanged a high five. We had our Body Sentence for enough:

E = point to your eyes
N= Nail your nose
O= Open your mouth
U= Under your chin
G=Give me your hand
H=High Five
You've got it!

Figure 41 enough

I asked the student for several weeks how to spell the word. He remembered how to write the sentence on his body to recall the word. Now, that I had a pilot Body Sentence, I had to come up with more.

In my role as a substitute teacher, the spelling list for the first-grade class I was teaching in had the word *could*. So many students forget that silent "L". *Would* and *should* similarly use that silent L. The students and I decided as a class that they knew the beginning letter. We filled in the rest of the sentences like this:

O= Open your mouth
U= draw a line Under your chin
L= Left arm bicep curl (makes an L shape)
D= Dig up dirt (make a motion like you are using a shovel)

I followed up by informing the teacher and asked a few weeks later how the spelling test went. All students recalled the Body Sentence. My next step was to make a phrase for each letter. On the next page are phrases for every letter of the alphabet:

Table 5 Body Sentence Alphabet

A	Apply deodorant	**N**	Nail your nose
B	Bounce the ball	**O**	Open your mouth
C	Comb your hair	**P**	Pinch your belly
D	Dig up dirt	**Q**	Quote the queen
E	Point to your Eyes	**R**	Run over the rock
F	Fold your hands	**S**	Sing to your shoulder
G	Give me your hand	**T**	Touch the ground
H	High five	**U**	Under your chin
I	Inch by inch on your arm	**V**	Vibrate your voice
J	Jump up to the sky	**W**	Whirl in a circle
K	Kick the ball	**X**	Cross it out
L	Bicep curl: child – left arm / Adult– right arm	**Y**	Yellow yawn
M	Muscle march	**Z**	Zip your coat

Please feel free to adjust phrases to best meet the needs of your student. Make all attempts to create an action using the letter of the alphabet in question. You can download a pdf version of the phrases at www. dysgraphiaconsultant.com. There is a small fee.

Picture Sentences

A picture sentence is a group of letter blends that represent homophone groups. These groups take the letter blend, create a picture of the blend, and use the picture to compare the similarities and difference. They creatively find ways to develop mental movements to assist children to memorize spelling lists through motivation.

One such combination is words that contain /ee/ or /ea/ and sound alike—blends such as *steel* and *steal*. By looking at the word as a picture the double e has a dotted line in the middle. Whereas, the /ea/ combination is a line followed by an arch.

Figure 42 steel vs steal

By moving the focus of spelling to a visual overview of the entire word, the visual memory of the word could become more automatic for students and fewer spelling errors could occur. As with Body Sentences, there needed to be a way of creating a mental movement to assist with the recall. This table is a summary of how to build on this memory process.

Table 6 Picture Sentence sample

ee Word	How to remember it	ea Word	How to remember it
deer	The antlers on this deer are straight.	dear	I am going to make hearts for my dear sweet Momma. The heart is curved which focuses on the bump.
feet	Your flat feet make a straight line.	feat	The courage to climb this hill and go down the other side is a great feat.
flee	Get out of here. Run in a straight line.	flea	A flea goes bouncing from animal to animal
heel	Strike your heel along the floor.	heal	A round band aid is all you need to heal that bump.
leek	The vegetable is straight and green.	leak	The drops of water from the leak are bouncing off the floor.
meet	My friend's eyes meet mine because we are both the same size. A straight line.	meat	The round steak is on my fork.
Pee	Pee straight into the toilet.	pea	The round pea shoots out from the vine.
Reed	The leaf on a reed is flat.	read	Read from the bottom of one page and bounce to the top of next page.
See	My friend's eyes meet mine because we are both the same size. A straight line.	sea	The waves of the sea were flat then rose into a curl for the surfer.
Seem	You seem flat today. You are not bouncing.	seam	The seam of that sleeve is straight until it reaches the shoulder. Then is curves around the arm.
Steel	A steel beam is straight.	steal	The robbers must jump through a window.
Tee	That golf tee is straight.	tea	Lift your tea bag into the cup
Week	days of the week are in a straight line	weak	That big bump in my arm is my bicep.

This list was taken from the third-grade curriculum. The list is not given to students all at once, but is broken up over several weeks. Other letter blends are intermingled within their weekly list.

Other homophone combinations that frustrate children include:

- Their/there/they're
- Two/too/to
- Right/write
- Piece/peace
- Bare/bear

Develop your own sentence pictures and share them with us at info@dysgraphiaconsultant.com. We would love to add more homophones.

Classroom Connection

Much of the classroom work integrates the entire curriculum today. Reading assignments are linked to social studies stories. Writing tasks are integrated into projects associated with the reading and social studies. Math and science can be linked in many ways as well. Parents may even need assistance with tasks at home and can incorporate writing practice into everyday activities.

Suppose you have a unit on land forms and masses. Could the student design a treasure map to accompany an island? He could dictate the ideas for the island into a recorder, and then play back the recorder adding one element at a time. Include details from class discussions. This assignment could also be linked to math or science by including an aspect of those subjects that is being taught in the classroom.

For students who love to build, have them generate the directions for a building design. They would be responsible to share the detailed directions with another student to create the building. Have them evaluate how each did at creating the design and implementing the directions.

Another idea could be to create a board game reflecting the subject. If you choose to do this activity with Social Studies vocabulary words or spelling, students could have to form words on the list to move their pawns.

Finally, help students generate integrative projects that coincide with the classroom. These could be floor maps, done individually or as a group project. To generate a map of the United States, one student could locate images on the internet and print out the states at a specific enlarged size. Another student could cut out the shapes, and then a third student could write the name of the state on the middle of the paper. The roles could be shifted periodically throughout the activity. For the student with dysgraphia, reduce their writing demands.

Everyday Living Activity

Parents can have their child help them prepare the grocery list. Record themselves speaking the list, and then the child can write the words from the recorded message.

Assistive Technologies Connection

Math difficulties have prompted assistive technologies to reinforce learning. Edu-tainment software programs such as *Math Blaster*, *Khan Academy*, and *EdSurge. com* are three examples.

In summary, adding motor movements that include the person will add a new dimension to educating children in word formation.

Chapter Sixteen

Encoding SFD

THE PRIMARY DIFFICULTIES that arise when a student has Sentence Formation Dysgraphia (SFD) are punctuation, capitalization, grammar errors, and run-on words. A run-on word is when there are no spaces between the words. An entire sentence might appear to be one long word. (This is different from the run-on sentence, where ideas from what would normally be several sentences run together into one sentence.) Sometimes there is a capital letter at the beginning of the sentence, but not always. Punctuation is often lacking. If the sentence structure is anything other than noun + verb, there are likely syntax errors. There are times in which single and plural nouns and verbs are misused. Their strengths are the same as WFD.

A low-tech method of helping these students is to have sample sentences as a visual cue with the capital letters, punctuation, and other pertinent features emphasized. Creating several choices of different sentence structures can help the student reinforce the similarities in the sentences.

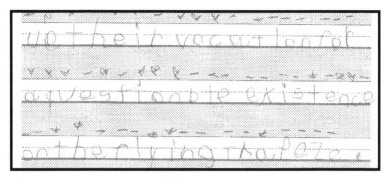

Figure 43 Run-on word sentence

Figure 44 Word spaces

To help avoid run-on words, a spacer can be used. The tool is removed after the word is written and moved to the end of the next word in the sentence. If used effectively, the student will see the visual break from one word to the next. The tools can be weaned to fingers over time and ultimately eliminated with successful trials of separated words. Manufacturers have versions that can be purchased online or at a store that sells educational materials. However, these spacers can be made from materials in your own home. Paper clips, stickers, pencils, craft sticks, or erasers can be used at the end of words to create a space between words for students.

After the sentence is written, have the student read their sentence back to himself aloud or another person. Have the student listen for errors in what is read. If the sentence was read aloud with the errors included, observe if he/she can pick up on the error auditorily. This process may take some practice for both the student and the adult, or a second student to pick up on the errors and emphasize them with the oral repetition of the student's sentence.

There are many high-tech features that have become mainstream in today's virtual environment.

Apps like *Co-Writer*, *Spell Better*, and sentence organizers can help students with sentence structure. However, *Microsoft Word* and *Google Docs* have improved the features on their platforms. These mainstream applications have speech to text features and word prediction. Please be advised that the application must become accustomed to the student's voice. Even the best apps available do not help every student. Activation of the features for the program may take several days to adjust to your student's intonations or articulation difficulties if they exist. *Proloquo2go* and *Word Power* are applications that cost money but are also speech to text software programs.

Chapter Seventeen

Encoding PFD

AS WITH THE areas of language dysgraphia, Paragraph Formation Dysgraphia (PFD) students demonstrate good oral skills but have weakness in writing. They hate graphic organizers usually because the space is too small for their comfort level with writing. Spelling rules, sequencing, organizing, and planning impact their writing style.

Once the sentence structure becomes integrated into the student's neural pathway, they need to begin writing paragraphs. A student at this level of dysgraphia may have significant executive function problems. Any combination of these and other methods that support executive function skills.

Some low-tech supports that you can supply for your student include note cards:

- Placing the dictated sentences on note cards. One sentence per card.

- o Have the student review the cards and place them to create the paragraph.

- o The student can copy the sentences from the cards to paper.

- o The note cards can include labels with copies of the student's writing paper if needed. The sentence can be written directly on the card if line placement is not a problem.

This technique takes the anxiety of trying to recall what the student said to answer the question.

Classroom Connection

For issues of reading comprehension, make copies of the passage and teach the student to highlight points. Then use the note card idea using the same colors for the sentences.

- Yellow = Main character

- Blue=Main idea

- Green=setting

- Orange=supporting text

WRITING BINDER

A writing binder is a collection of supports for Language Arts, Math, Social Studies, Science, and any other subject that needs assistance. Sample sentences, math formulas, and other materials are included. Some of the additional items can be a noun bank, a verb bank, transition words, social skills interactions, and visual schedules. This binder is student-specific.

PRERECORD LECTURES AND ASSIGNMENT RESPONSES

By recording a lecture in class or student's response to an assignment, the comments can be written by listening to brief segments. The note card method or speech to text dictation method can be used for this purpose. Please note, that these pre-recorded assignment responses are like a brainstorming or first draft. Review of the content for completeness must be done. Also, taking notes from a pre-recorded lecture can be time consuming. Some students simply need to hear the recording to process the content.

TRANSITION WORD BANK

More complex styles of writing require transition words like 'for example,' 'for instance,' 'moreover,' 'like,' etc. Placing a list of these words in the writing binder can help students advance their writing style.

Assistive Technology Connection

This form of dysgraphia is best supported by assistive technology. The programs discussed in Sentence Dysgraphia section will also support this type of dysgraphia.

In summary, paragraph dysgraphia is best supported with external supports to alleviate anxiety and avoid the brain break that occurs between oral and written language. Several low tech and high-tech options are available to assist your students. Be open to trying new methods with various emerging technologies. Parents and teachers should work together to develop the best strategies for students. Always remember to take all strategies back to school administrators. Don't hesitate to be a world changer, one student at a time. Don't ever give up. Keep supporting kids!

I hope that this book helped explain how dysgraphia impacts students in the classroom and provides you with inclusive strategies that can be implemented across your entire curriculum. Thank you for reading. For more information and more strategies go to www.dysgraphiaconsultant.com and take our question-naire to determine the type of dysgraphia your student may have and strategies to maximize their learning experience.

References

Adam, M. (2015). *Dysgraphia*. Retrieved from Special Needs Project: https://specialneedsprojecteec424. weebly.com/dysgraphia.html

AlleyDog. (n. d.). *Online glossary*. Retrieved from Alleydog.com: https://www.alleydog.com/glossary/ definition-cit.php?term=Encoding

Amen, D., & Amen, T. (2017). Brain health. *The SuperHero You Conference December 9, 2016*. Los Angeles, CA: Jim Kwik.

American Psychiatric Association (APA). (2013). *Diagnostic and statistical manual of mental disorders (DSM-V)* (Fifth ed.). Washington D.C.: American Psychaitric Association.

AOTA. (2014). *Occupational therapy practice framework: Domain and process* (3rd ed., Vol. 68). Bethesda, MD: American Occupational Therapy Association. doi:10.5014/ajot.2014.682006OTPF 3rd edition

Ayers, A. J. (1979). *Sesnory integration and the child*. Los Angeles, CA: Western Psychological Services.

Bear, D. R., Invernizzi, M., Templeton, S., & Jonston, F. (2016). *Words their way: Word study for phonics, vocabulary, and spelling instruction.* (Kindle ed.). Upper Saddle River, NJ: Pearson Education, Inc.

Berninger, W. W., & Wolf, B. (2018). *Understanding dysgraphia fact sheet.* Baltimore, MD: International Dyslexia Association. Retrieved from https://dyslexiaida.org/understanding-dysgraphia/

Boundless Chemistry. (2014, Nov 25). *Accuracy, Precision, and Error.* Retrieved 4 19, 2015, from www.boundless.com: https://www.boundless.com/chemistry/textbooks/boundless-chemistry-textbook/introduction-to-chemistry-1/measurement-uncertainty-30/accuracy-precision-and-error-190-3706/

BrainPages. (2018). *Can you spot the ten faces in the tree?* Retrieved from BrainPages: http://brainpages.org/can-you-spot-the-ten-faces-in-the-tree/

Brant, N. (2014). *Dysgraphia: A parent's guide to understanding dysgrapia and helping a dysgraphia child* (Kindle ed.). Amazon.

Bryce, B., & Stephens, B. (2014). *The dysgraphia sourcebook: Everything you need to help your child* (Kindle ed.). Amazon.

Canfield, J. (2017). Focused mindset. *The SuperHero You Conference December 9, 2016.* Los Angeles, CA: Jim Kwik.

Dawson, P., & Guare, R. (2010). *Executive skills in children and adolescents: A practical guide to assessments and intervention.* (2nd, Trans.) New York, NY: Guilford Press.

Deng, W., Aimone, J. B., & Gage, F. H. (2010). New neurons and new memories: How does adult hippocampal neurogenesis affect learning and memory? *Neuroscience, 11*(5), 339-350. doi:10.1038/nrn2822

References

Dolch, E. W. (1936). basic sight vocabulary. *The Elementary School Journal, 36*(6), 456-460. doi:10.1086/457353

Duncan, A. (2015, October 5). This LD Awareness Month: U.S. Department of Education recognizes the 1 in 5. Washington D. C.: National Center for Learning Disabilities. Retrieved from https://www.ncld.org/ archives/action-center/what-we-ve-done/this-l d-awareness-month-u-s-department-of-education- recognizes-the-1-in-5

Dunn, W. (2015, 4 18). *Introduction to Sensory Processing Concepts.* Retrieved from Sensoty Processing in Everyday Life: http://classes.kumc. edu/sah/resources/sensory_processing/learning_ opportunities/concepts/sp_concepts_main.htm

Dunn, W. (2015, 4 18). *Winifred Dunn's Bio.* Retrieved 4 18, 2015, from University of Kansas: http://www.kumc.edu/ school-of-health-professions/occupational-therapy- education/our-faculty/dunn.html

Dyslexia Literacy and Clinical Services (SPELD). (2014). *Teaching written expression.* Retrieved from SPELD: https://dsf. net.au/teaching-written-expression/

Eckersley, S. (2012, August 4). Spatial awareness. *Occupational therapy for children.* Retrieved from http://occupationaltherapy forchildren.over-blog. com/article-spatial-awareness-108726104.html

Eckert, M. A., Keren, N. I., Roberts, D. R., Calhoun, V. D., & Harris, K. C. (2010, Mar 8). Age-related changes in processing speed: unique contributions of cerebellar and prefrontal cortex. *Frontiers in human neuroscience, 4*(Article 10). doi:10.3389/neuro.09.010.2010

Educational Psycologist. (2016, January 23). Diagnosis of dysgraphia: Assessment and diagnosis. Retrieved from http://www. educational-psychologist.co.uk/sen-reso urces-blog/2016/1/22/cannot-pass-the-knowledg e-of-life-and-language-in-the-uk-test-knoll-1

Erickson, M. (2015, October 5). Learning disabilities awareness month: Beyond the dys in dyslexia. Washington D. C.: U. S. Department of Education. Retrieved from https://sites.ed.gov/osers/2015/10/this-ld-awareness-month-beyond-the-dys-in-dyslexia/

Eriksson, P., Perfilieva, E., Bjork-Eriksson, T., Alborn, A., Nordborg, C., Peterson, D., & Gage, F. (1998). Neurogenesis in the adult human hippocampus. *Nature Medicine, 4,* 1313-1317.

Eye Can Learn b. (n. d.). *Visual Closure.* Retrieved from Eye Can Learn: http://eyecanlearn.com/perception/closure/

Eye Can Learn c. (n. d.). *Visual Figure Ground.* Retrieved from Eye Can Learn: http://eyecanlearn.com/perception/figure-ground/

Eye Can Learn. (n.d.). *Visual form constancy.* Retrieved from EyeCanLearn.com: http://eyecanlearn .com/perception/ constancy/

Fischman, M. G. (2007). Motor Learning and Control: Foundations of Kinesiolopgy, Defining the Academic Core. *American Academy of Kinesiology and Physical Education, 59,* 67-76. Retrieved 4 19, 2015, from http://www.humankinetics.com/acucustom/sitename/Documents/DocumentItem/6990.pdf

Fry, E. (1980). The new instant word list. *The Reading Teacher, 34*(3), 284-289.

Galvin, S., & Pooler, P. (2016). *Visual perception and spatial relationships/position in space.* Retrieved from Tools to grow OT: http://www.toolsto growot. com /therapy-resources/visual-perception/spatial-relationsposition-in-space

Gardner, B., Lally, P., & Wardle, J. (2012). Making health habitual: The psycology pf "habit-formation" and general practice. *British Journal of General Practice,* 62(605), 664-666. doi:10.3399/bjgp12X659466

References

Gundersen, K. (2016). Muscle memory and a new hypertrophy. *Journal of Experimental Biology, 219,* 245-242. doi:doi:10.1242/jeb.124495

Hain, T. C., & Helminski, J. O. (2007). Anatomy and Physiology of the normal vestibular system. In S. Herdman, *Vestibular rehabilitation* (3rd edition ed., pp. 2-18). Philadelphia: F. A. Davis Company.

HPS. (2018). *What is dysgraphia?* Retrieved from handwriting-solutions.com: http://www.handwriting-solutions.com/dysgraphia.asp

Jones, S. (1999). *Dysgraphia accommodations and modifications.* Retrieved from LD Online: http://www.ldonline.org/article/6202

Karnik, D. J., & Karnik, J. D. (2012). *Dysgraphia* (Kindle ed.). Amazon.

Kelly, V. E. (Spring 2008). Postural Control. *University of Washington Class Outline Rehab 442.* Retrieved 4 19, 2015

Laberge, M. (2015, 4 19). *Eye-hand coordination.* (I. Advameg, Editor) Retrieved from Encylclopedia of Children's Health: http://www.healthofchildren.com/G-H/Hand-Eye-Coordination.html

Larson, D. (2017). Study skills. *The SuperHero You Conference December 9, 2016.* Los Angeles, CA: Jim Kwik.

Learn, E. C. (n.d.). *Visual Closure.* Retrieved from Eye Can Learn.

Marianek, J. (2017, October 29). *Brand new: Opinions on coroprate and brand identity work ToyRUs and BabiesRUslogos.* Retrieved from UnderConsideration.com: http://www.underconsideration.com/brandnew/archives/toys_r_us_grows.php#.V9xJmZgrKUk

Mastin, L. (2018). *Memory Encoding.* Retrieved from The Human Memory: http://www.human-memory.net/processes_encoding.html

175

McDermott, K. B., & Roediger, H. L. (2018). Memory (encoding, storage, retreival). In R. Biswas-Diener, & E. Diener, *Noba Textbook Series: Psychology.* Champaign, IL: DEF Publishers. doi:nobaproject.com

MedicineNet. (2016). *Definition of autonomic nervous system.* Retrieved from MedicineNet: http://www.medicinenet.com /script/main/art. asp?articlekey=2403

MedicineNet. (2016, May 13). *Definition of visceral.* Retrieved from MedicineNet: http://www.medicine net .com/script /main/art.asp?articlekey =18275

MedicineNet. (2017, January 24). *Definition of neuroplasticity.* Retrieved from MedicineNet.com: http://www. medicinenet.com/ script/main/art. asp?articlekey=40362

MedicineNet. (2018, March 6). *Definition of autonomic nervous system.* Retrieved from MedicineNet: http://www.medicinenet.com /script/main/art. asp?articlekey=2403

Merriam-Webster. (2017). *Definition of neurotypical.* Retrieved from Merriam Webster Disctionary: www. merriam-webster.com/dictionary/neurotypical

Miller, L. J. (2015, 4 18). *About SPD.* Retrieved from SPD Foundation: http://spdfoundation.net/about-sensor y-processing-disorder/

Moskowitz, B. (2015). *Size matters handwriting intruction manual.* Villanova, PA: Self-published.

Norkin, C. C., & Levangie, P. K. (1992). *Joint structure & function* (2nd edition ed.). Philadelphia: F. A. Davis Company.

Olsen, J. Z., & Knapton, E. F. (2008). *Handwriting without tears: Pre-K teacher's guide.* Cabin John, MD: Self-published.

Parham, L. D., & Mailloux, Z. (2005). Chapter 11: Sensory Integration. In J. Case-Smith, *Occupational therapy* for children (Fifth edition ed., pp. 356-409). St. Louis, Missouri: Elsevier Mosby.

Parham, L. D., & Mailloux, Z. (2005). Sensory integration. In J. Case-Smith, *Occupational Therapy for Children* (5th ed., pp. 356-411). St. Louis, MO: Elseivier, Inc.

Pedretti, L. W. (1990). Evaluation of sensation and treatment of sensory dysfunction. In L. W. Pedretti, & B. Zoltan, *Occupational therapy: practice skills for physical dysfunction* (3rd edition ed., p. 186). St. Louis, Missouri: C. V. Mosby Company.

Pfeiffer, B., Moskowitz, B., Paoletti, A., Brusilovskiy, E., Zylstra, S. E., & Murray, T. (2015, June). Brief Report - Developmental Test of Visual–Motor Integration (VMI): An effective outcome measure for handwriting interventions for. *American Journal of Occupational Therapy, 69*(4), 6904350010. doi:10.5014/ajot.2015.015826

Pollock, A. S., Durward, B. R., Rowe, P. J., & Paul, J. P. (2000, Aug 14). What is balance? *Clinical Rehabilitation, 4*, 402-6.

Purves, D., Augustine, G. A., Fitzpatrick, D., Hall, W. C., LaMantia, A., & White, L. E. (2012). Central visual pathways. In D. Purves, G. A. Augustine, D. Fitzpatrick, W. C. Hall, A. LaMantia, & L. E. White, *Neuroscience* (pp. 257-276). Sunderland, MA: Sinauer Associates, Inc.

Randhawa, M. (2013). *Vision Therapy*. Retrieved from Double Vision: www.visiontherapy.ca/double-vision.html

Roley, S. S., Mailloux, Z., Parham, L. D., Schaaf, R. C., Lane, C. J., & Cermak, S. (2015). Sensory integration and praxis patterns in children with autism. *American Journal of Occupational Therapy, 69*, 6901220010. doi:http://dx.doi.org/10.5014/ajot.2015.012476

Roll 2 Roll Technologies, Inc. (2017). *Accuracy, precision, linearity, and resolution web guiding understanding terminology*. Retrieved from r2r. tech: https://r2r.tech/articles/accuracy-precisio n-linearity-and-resolution-web-guiding-unders tanding-terminology

Rouse, M. (2005). *Encoding and decoding*. Retrieved from TechTarget.com: http:// searchnetworking. techtarget.com/definition/ encoding-and-decoding

Schneck, C. (2005). Visual Perception. In J. Case-Smith, *Occupational Therapy for Children* (pp. 412-446). St. Louis, MO: Elsevier Mosby.

Section 504 of the Rehabilitation Act of. (1973). as ammended, *29 U. S. C. 794*.

Sheiman, M. (2002). *Understanding and managing vision deficits* (2nd ed.). Philadelphia, PA: Slack, Inc.

Taylor, S. J. (2016, October). OptiMind Coaching Neuroscience Made Simple Online Course. Austin, TX.

USDOE. (2014). *Related Service Providers, Section 300.34*. Retrieved from Individuals with Disability Act: https://sites.ed.gov/idea/regs/b/a/300.34

VanHoorn, J., Maathuis, C., Peters, L., & Hadders-Algra, M. (2010). Handwriting, visuomotor integration, and neurologocal condition at school age. *Developmental Medicine & Child Neurology, 52*, 941-947. doi:10.1111/j.1469-8749.2010.03715.x

Zwicker, J., & Harris, S. (2009). A reflection on motor learning theory in pediatric occupational therapy proactice. *Canadian Journal of Occupational Therapy, 76*(1), 29-37. doi:10.1177/000841740907600108

APPENDICES

Appendix A

Resources for Brain Development

Dr. Daniel Amen
http://danielamenmd.com
TEDx Talk: https://www.youtube.com/
watch?v=esPRsT-lmw8

Book Title	Year Published
Feel Better Fast and Make It Last: Unlock Your Brain's Healing Potential to Overcome Negativity, Anxiety, Anger, Stress, and Trauma	2018
Memory Rescue: Supercharge Your Brain, Reverse Memory Loss, and Remember What Matters Most	2017
The Brain Warrior's Way: Ignite Your Energy and Focus, Attack Illness and Aging, Transform Pain into Purpose	2016
Change Your Brain, Change Your Life: Revised and Expanded Edition: The Breakthrough Program for Conquering Anxiety, Depression, Anger and Obsessiveness	2016

Use Your Brain to Change Your Age:
Secrets to Look, Feel and Think Younger
Every Day   2014

Healing ADD Revised Edition: The
Breakthrough Program that Allows You to
See and Heal the 7 Types of ADD   2013

Change Your Brain, Change Your Body   2010

The Amen Solution: The Brain Healthy Way
to Lose Weight and Keep It Off   2011

Plus, several more books that have been
co-authored with other people

Dr. Mark Hyman
http://drhyman.com/
TEDmed talk: https://www.youtube.com/
watch?v=IhkLcpJTV9M

Book Title	Year Published
Food: What the Heck Should I Eat?	2018
Eat Fat, Get Thin: Why the Fat We Eat Is the Key to Sustained Weight Loss and Vibrant Health	2016
The Blood Sugar Solution 10-Day Detox Diet: Activate Your Body's Natural Ability to Burn Fat and Lose Weight Fast	2014
The Blood Sugar Solution: The UltraHealthy Program for Losing Weight, Preventing Disease, and Feeling Great Now!	2012
Until It Hurts: America's Obsession with Youth Sports and How It Harms Our Kids	2010
The UltraMind Solution: Fix Your Broken Brain by Healing Your Body First	2008

Appendix B

References for Sensory Processing Disorder

Book Title	Year Published
The Out of Sync Child by Carol Stock Kranowitz	2006
Raising a Sensory Smart Child by Lindsey Biel and Nancy Peske	2009
Sensory Processing 101 by Dayna Abraham and Claire Heffron	2005
Sensational Kids by Lucy Jane Miller	2014
Sensory Integration and the Child. The 25th Anniversary edition	2004
Sensory Integration and the Child by A. Jean Ayers	1979
The Out of Sync Child: Recognizing and Coping with Sensory Processing Disorder by Carol Kranowitz and Lucy Jane Miller	2005
A Buffet of Sensory Interventions: Solutions for Middle and High School Students with Autism Spectrum Disorders by Susan Culp	2011

Appendix C

Handwriting Resources for Students

Manuscript

LouAnne Audette and Anne Karson
www.gettingitwrite2.com
Getting it Write

Linda Becht
www.atclearning.com
The Sensible Pencil

Beverly Moskowitz
www.RealOTSolutions.com
Size Matters Handwriting Program

Jan Olsen
www.HWTears.com
Handwriting without Tears

Charles Trafford and Rand Nelson
www.peterson-handwriting.com
Petersen Directed Handwriting

Cursive

Mary Benbow
www.proedinc.com
Loops and other groups

Carson-Dellosa Publishing
https://www.carsondellosa.com
Brighter Child Cursive Handwriting Workbook

Kama Einhorn
www.scholastic.com
Cursive Writing Made Easy & Fun!

Appendix D

What Does the Law Say?

Now that I have explained what is happening in the brain and body of students with dysgraphia, let's review what the law states about OT services in the public school. Please note, this law is not exactly applied the same in private, charter, and other types of school systems. However, some of the material may still help you better understand how referrals are and can be made.

Are you aware that most teachers only have one course in reading literacy for each age group in an elementary education four-year program? One, that's it. They are educated in the basics. To further explore reading, teachers must attend graduate school to become reading specialists. There are many children out there with difficulties, but most school districts only have one reading specialist on staff. The science behind reading is better understood today than it was 20-30 years ago. Demands on students are also significantly different than they were 20-30 years ago. Reading difficulties bring referrals within the schools for other professionals to assist with the child's education. These staff members can work alongside OTs to maximize a child's performance in the classroom.

The law that governs how this assistance is rendered is the Individuals with Disabilities Education Act (IDEA) of 2004 (USDOE, 2014). According to the IDEA, "public education is designed to prepare children to obtain further education as well as employability and independent citizens who contribute to the overall benefit of society" (USDOE, 2014).

Furthermore, Section 504 of the Rehabilitation Act of 1973 protects the rights of individuals with disabilities in programs and activities that receive federal financial assistance, which includes federal funds. Section 504 of the Rehabilitation Act of 1973 provides that:

> "No otherwise qualified individual with a disability in the United States . . . shall, solely by reason of her or his disability, be excluded from the participation in, be denied the benefits of, or be subjected to discrimination under any program or activity receiving Federal financial assistance . . ." Another way of stating this quote is that all children are guaranteed a Free Appropriate Public Education (FAPE). Children that are found to have a disability or special needs, whether visible or not visible, will need special learning instruction to prepare them to meet this criterion. (Section 504 of the Rehabilitation Act of, 1973)

The statue relating to related services includes:

"(26) Related services. --

(A) In general.--The term `related services' means transportation, and such developmental, corrective, and other supportive services (including speech-language pathology and audiology services, interpreting services, psychological services, physical and occupational therapy, recreation, including therapeutic recreation, social work services, school nurse services designed to enable a child with a disability to receive a free appropriate public education as described in the individualized education program of the child, counseling services, including rehabilitation counseling, orientation and mobility services, and medical services, except that such medical services shall be for diagnostic and evaluation purposes only) as may be required to assist a child with a disability to benefit from special education, and includes the early identification and assessment of disabling conditions in children.

(B) Exception. --The term does not include a medical device that is surgically implanted, or the replacement of such device, (USDOE, 2014)

As you can see from this excerpt of the law, related services go beyond the school psychologist and occupational therapist. IDEA is important because it regulates what these services can do in public schools. Occupational therapists (OTs) analyze why the handwriting and other behaviors may be difficult for a child. Handwriting and sensory processing disorders are the primary reasons for referral of occupational therapy evaluations and services. IDEA covers OT services and states that the service must help a child engage in their education. An OT does have some limitations, but as long as the use of the OT is preparing a student for college or career, OT services must be provided (USDOE, 2014); (AOTA, 2014).

Kindergarten through second grade is the first block of identification in the public-school system. You may have been fortunate that your child was identified during this time. If so, you have a jump start, as some children are not identified with learning disabilities until middle school.

On the other hand, you may have a child that has been tested and does not qualify for special education services under the IDEA. Your child, no matter his or her age, still has the right to a Free Appropriate Public Education (FAPE). Keep fighting for your child. Remember, you are not alone.

Another note: Not all children with special needs have learning disabilities. There is also a category of students contained in the law that have special needs: gifted students. These students are considered to have high IQs. They have their own requirements for a FAPE. Please note that children with gifted IQs may also have learning disabilities.

Appendix E

Occupational Therapy Goals, Accommodations, and Modifications

Since the regulations state that occupational therapy through the school system must serve a child demonstrating a delay of at least one standard deviation and that the delay is limiting the child's ability to engage in a Free Appropriate Public Education (FAPE), it is necessary to review what that looks like in the Individualized Education Program (IEP).

A comprehensive occupational therapy evaluation includes an informal portion, some standardized assessments, and other assessments that provide a percentage. The evaluation should cover sensory processing screening from at least two adults who work with the student, a standardized visual-motor processing assessment that reports on specific subcategories, a handwriting assessment of print and cursive handwriting as appropriate for age and the child's knowledge, an upper extremity assessment, gross and fine motor skills, and activities of daily living. The overall goal of an educational occupational therapy evaluation is to determine a child's areas of educational need. This makes it so the child obtains a FAPE through appropriate related services and to make recommendations to address specially designed instruction, so the child can fully participate in his or her education.

Standardized occupational therapy assessments are typically normed on scale that includes the mean as 100, with a standard deviation of 15. That means that the typical child will score between 85-115. Scores below 85 are greater than one standard deviation from the mean. Scores greater than 115 also exceed one standard deviation from the mean. Scores 116 or higher indicate that the child is gifted in the specific area, while scores less than 85 indicate that the child has a disability in the test.

Still other occupational therapy assessments use scaled scores to explain the assessment results. Typically, a scaled score mean is 10 and one standard deviation from the mean is 3. Therefore, children with typical scores range from 7 to 13, less than 7 is a disability, and above 13 represents a student who is gifted in that area of the assessment.

The comprehensive evaluation should consist of an informal section. In this section, the occupational therapist gathers data from resources such as parents and teachers through interviews and/or general demographic surveys. These surveys may include behaviors that occur at home including homework, nutrition, sleep schedules, and family dynamics.

Formal assessments can include a sensory processing screening, a visual processing assessment, a handwriting assessment, upper extremity performance, gross and fine motor skills, and activities of daily living. There are several assessment questionnaires that are completed by the teacher and parent as well as other professionals. Other assessments have standardized forms that are completed with the student. In addition, the therapist may also ask the student to complete tasks that could occur in the classroom that are observations of the child's abilities, but do not have a formal standardization assessment that is included. One example of an observed activity is putting on a coat.

From the evaluation, the occupational therapist creates a report and intervention plan based on two primary goals. The first goal is to determine the child's areas of need that is preventing them from achieving a Free Appropriate Public Education (FAPE) (USDOE, 2014). The second goal is to make appropriate recommendations to address specially designed instruction or accommodations and modifications so that the child can fully participate in their education. Goals are written to support that area of need, and are created to be child specific for the IEP. Included in the next section is an example of an OT goal for the different areas assessed.

Example of a Goal for Form Constancy

[The student] will identify similarities and differences among shapes and symbols to increase participation in reading and handwriting to demonstrate progress similar to peers over the duration of the IEP year.

Example Goals for Orientation, Laterality, or Directionality

[The student] will write all capital and lowercase letters and numbers in the appropriate direction to demonstrate similar progress to peers during the duration of the IEP year.

[The student] will use adaptive paper (include type here) using appropriate sizing and letter placement without reversals to be equivalent to peers over the duration of the IEP year.

Example Goal for Visual Figure Ground

[The student] will be able to copy [# of sentences] with 80% accuracy and precision using a [source to copy from] while decreasing font size and type from [insert font size and type that student can use now] to 12-point Arial or Times Roman.

Example Goal for Visual Closure

[The student] will fill in the blanks on his/her worksheet in the space provided by the manufacturer using [accommodation] to become similar to peers over the duration of this IEP year.

Example Goal for Convergence/ Divergence Insufficiency

[The student] will copy homework assignments from board into agenda within [fill in # minutes] to become comparable to peers over the duration of this IEP year.

Example Goal for Fine Motor Skills

[The student] will pick up [an object] and manipulate it in his/her hand to be able to use it like their peers over the duration of this IEP year.

The object in question could be a manipulative for math, a die, a pencil, or an eraser. It could also include fasteners for clothing like zippers and buttons.

Example Goals for Activities of Daily Living

[The student] will put his/her jacket on and off in a time similar to peers over the duration of this IEP year.

[The student] will pull up/down his/her own pants when toileting over the duration of this IEP year. There are many more varieties to these goals to make them unique to the specific child. When relating goals to the classroom, some language that teachers may use to write a goal include grade level and proficiency, areas related to the subject matter of the goal, and a measure of a standardized assessment used in the academic setting. These standardized assessments might not record similar numbers to the ones discussed earlier in this chapter. Ask if you do not understand how the evaluator is coming up with their data.

Examples of Specially Designed Instruction

After a goal is created, there also needs to be an accommodation or modification to the student's regular education curriculum to reflect how the staff member will be working with him/her to improve his/her FAPE. Accommodations and modifications are included in the Specially Designed Instruction portion:

- Preferential seating near front, back, near door, or near window
- Whatever posture is necessary for success

Use of the IEP paperwork. Some common accommodations include:

- Increased time to complete assignments
- Change assignment deadlines
- Use resource teacher to assist with organization of material

- Provide partially completed notes – add fill in the blanks with adaptive paper accommodation

- Offer a scribe to write verbatim what child says

- Teach keyboarding alongside handwriting

- Reduce copying requirements

  - Allow student to turn in paper with edit markings

- Have a fellow student proofread work for student

- Have a student buddy to help make sure homework is going home

- Adaptive paper and pencil

- Adaptive writing surface

  - Elevated surface

  - Blotter surface

  - Extra paper

- Changing format

  - Oral report

  - Power Point

  - Fewer details

  - Record oral answers

    - Scribe each sentence on note cards

    - Have student arrange and copy appropriate note cards

  - Create outline for each paragraph

  - Provide a finished sample of work

  - Positive behavioral support

- Teacher-parent communication book
- Sign homework
- Hand in homework via email
- Daily visual for expectations
- Visual of class rules on desk
- Highlight notes in textbook, if allowed by school

For students that do well with visual-spatial information, but have difficulty with recall, they may benefit from a writing binder. This binder includes reference material of previously learned lessons that can be used with a visual cue. Binders could include:

- Model of manuscript and cursive writing
- Have template for heading location to hand in work
- Provide examples of writing stages
  - Brainstorming
  - Drafting
  - Editing
  - Proofreading
  - Copying
  - Graphic additions
- Visual schedule
- Math formulas

Be receptive to child's needs and create a binder to fit them.

Some accommodations to fit math alignment include the use of graph paper. ½-inch graph paper for younger students and ¼-inch for more proficient writers.

Physical environment within the classroom is important to consider. Some accommodations to assist students include:

- Move seat manipulatives

- Hands-on projects

- Quiet Zone

- Use of headphones

- Rest/walking breaks

- Pace the assignments

- Offer a word bank

Accommodations

I've been asked repeatedly about using keyboarding as an accommodation for writing. Motor theory states that you need to use the pathway, or you will lose it. Although I am an advocate to keyboarding as an accommodation, I must emphasize that keyboarding is **not** a replacement for writing. Different neural pathways are created when writing. Decide what is necessary and beneficial to practice with writing and use keyboarding as a supplemental accommodation, not a replacement. Here are some websites that include typing practice and training.

- *Keyboarding with Tears*

- *Typing.com*
- *Nessy.com*
- *DanceMatTyping.com*
- *TypingClub.com*

In addition to keyboarding, there are other assistive technologies that can support students in both Mac, iOS, PC, and Android platforms. These technologies have become part of our everyday lives, and so should be incorporated in educational supplements. Text to speech and speech to text platforms are included in many software programs today. Even *Google* and *Microsoft Office* document files have this feature. Quick notetaking and reminder features are also included. *Google Keep* and *Prizmo Go* are examples. The Pixel 2 allows you to squeeze the phone and *Google* will take a message for you, search your contacts and make a phone call or text message. Another program that may be helpful is *Co-Writer*. This program helps students restructure sentences while writing.

A Message from Cheri

Thank you for your interest in my book and education programs. My mission is to have the term dysgraphia known around the world. I want this specific learning disability to be recognized so that we can change the lives of children and improve the educational system.

Cheri's Contact Information:
Website: www.dysgraphiaconsultant.com
LinkedIn: https://www.linkedin.com/in/cdotterer/
Facebook page: https://www.facebook.com/
DysgraphiaConsultant/
Facebook Group:
https://www.facebook.com/groups/HWBBD

About the Author

Cheri is a dysgraphia consultant who helps teachers, occupational therapists, parents, and other related service providers understand handwriting issues, so they can transform a child's ability to learn.

With over 20 years of occupational therapy experience, author and mentor Cheri Dotterer is zealous about how we learn. She worked in many environments, including acute care, skilled nursing homes, home care, and most recently school-based pediatrics. Pediatrics has always been her passion and love. Her favorite part of practice is seeing the "light bulb" go on in the mind of parents, teachers, and children. Cheri has made it her mission to have the dysgraphia known around the world. She wants this specific learning disability recognized so that we can change the lives of children and improve the educational system.

Cheri brings with her years of research and education. She earned a Bachelor of Science degree in both Biochemistry and Occupational Therapy and later a Master of Science in Occupational Therapy. In addition, she holds a certificate as a Board-Certified Educational Advocate and Neuroscience Coach. Furthermore, she has worked alongside several universities creating unique experiences for OT students and organizations in the practice of occupational therapy through adjunct faculty and guest lecturer positions.

Cheri sees the world from a non-traditional perspective. She has a private practice in Pennsylvania and lives with her husband of 28 years, their two children, and their cat, Snowball.

Previous Teaching Experiences
University Faculty
Pennsylvania State University
Alvernia University
Misericordia University

University/College/Technical School Guest Lecturer
Pennsylvania State University
Temple University
Salus University
Berks Technical Institute

Other Speaking Locations
Berks County Autism Society
National Special Education Advocacy Institute
Pennsylvania Occupational Therapy Association
Chester County Right to Education Task Force
ARC of Chester County, PA
Hamburg Area Middle School
Pennsylvania Education for All Coalition

This publication accompanies the course titled *Handwriting Brain-Body DisConnect Workshop.*

Author: Cheri L. Dotterer, MS, OTR/L

Illustrator: Alyssa Marzili

Editors: William Houlette, Bethany Peat

Book cover design: Arrow Designs

Publisher: Author Academy Elite: Powell, OH

Distribution: Ingram Spark, Inc.

Paperback: 978-1-64085-391-1
Hardback: 978-1-64085-392-8
E-book: 978-1-64085-393-5
Library of Congress Control Number: 2018953205

Every effort has been made to contact copyright holders and to ensure that all the information presented is correct. Some of the facts in this volume may be subject to debate or dispute. If proper copyright acknowledgment has not been made, or for clarifications and corrections, please contact the publishers and we will correct the information in future reprintings, if any.

Here's a link that you
can share with your
colleagues and friends.

Types of Dysgraphia

dysgraphiaconsultant.com

Inside, there is a free
webinar that describes
the basics of the Types
of Dysgraphia.

www.dysgraphiaconsultant.thinkific.com

You've read the book.

Are you ready to experience a calmer classroom or home?

Get your continuing education credits here!

Handwriting: Brain-Body DisConnect

dysgraphiaconsultant.com

www.dysgraphiaconsultant.thinkific.com

Book Two Coming Soon......

Topic: Dyscalculia

Promoting FUNctional living through rhythmic expression

Serving
schools/learning centers
seniors
special needs/support groups
adult and community education
programs

Jorge Ochoa, OTR/L
San Antonio, TX
www.TamboRhythms.com

Has appeared in
San Antonio Express News
Our Kids San Antonio
Natural Awakenings
The Autism Notebook publications

Made in the USA
Columbia, SC
07 May 2019